Lore

of the

Ghost

The Origins of the Most Famous
Ghost Stories Throughout the World

Brian Haughton

Illustrated by Daniele Serra

New Page Books
A Division of Career Press, Inc.
Franklin Lakes, NJ

LORE OF THE GHOST
EDITED BY KATE HENCHES
TYPESET BY MICHAEL FITZGIBBON
Cover design by Lu Rossman/Digi Dog Design NY
Cover Art by Ian Daniels
Interior Art by Daniele Serra
Printed in the U.S.A. by Book-mart Press

To order this title, please call toll-free 1-800-CAREER-1 (NJ and Canada: 201-848-0310) to order using VISA or MasterCard, or for further information on books from Career Press.

The Career Press, Inc., 3 Tice Road, PO Box 687,
Franklin Lakes, NJ 07417
www.careerpress.com
www.newpagebooks.com

Library of Congress Cataloging-in-Publication Data

Haughton, Brian, 1964–
    Lore of the ghost : the origins of the most famous ghost stories throughout the world
/ by Brian Haughton,
        p. cm.
    Includes index.
    ISBN 978-1-60163-024-7
        1. Ghost stories—History and criticism. I. Title.

PN3435.H38 2009
398.25094—dc22

                                                                        2008025460

Dedication

for my family.

Contents

Introduction

Ghosts are perhaps the most controversial and the most widely reported of all anomalous phenomenon. But although ghostly visitors are sighted in the thousands all throughout the world and "true" ghost tales are hugely popular, the whole subject of ghost lore is widely misinterpreted and misunderstood. The majority of people are familiar with at least one local or national ghost story, but the role of folklore, folk tales, and urban legends in connection with the supernatural is rarely touched upon outside of academic journals. However the connection between folklore and allegedly true accounts of the supernatural is an important and extremely relevant one. Does this mean then that we can interpret the endless streams of headless horsemen, phantom nuns and monks, spectral armies, ghostly Roman legionaries, vanishing hitchhikers, black dogs, and white ladies as figures of folklore and urban legend rather than physical reality? Perhaps this is to oversimplify a complex phenomenon, but certainly the development of folk beliefs through the centuries has affected the way in which we report and interpret ghostly phenomena.

Every culture has its own particular kind of ghost lore, and some, like England, have a history of phantom reports stretching back to pre-Medieval times. Generally, "true" accounts of ghosts and hauntings can be dated back at least as far as classical Greece (5th–4th centuries BC) and the genre shows no signs of waning in the 21st century. But what exactly is a ghost? In general, the term is used to describe the appearance of the souls or spirits of the dead, while the word *haunting* signifies the recurring manifestation of a ghost witnessed by someone in a certain location. A ghost is usually described as similar in appearance, if not identical, to the dead person when they were living. However, not all hauntings involve apparitions. They may be auditory (relating to the sense of hearing) or olfactory (relating to the sense of smell), types of phenomena most frequently reported in poltergeist cases.

But even with such apparently safe definitions we are not always on sure ground. As Owen Davies points out in his authoritative *The Haunted: A Social History of Ghosts* (Palgrave Macmillan, 2007), in the past it was fairies that were believed to haunt certain locations, which would seem to indicate an origin in folklore and legend for the idea of haunted spots. Writing in his classic work on fairy lore *The Secret Commonwealth of Elves, Fauns, and Fairies* (1661) the Scottish antiquarian the Reverend Robert Kirk noted that it was a popular idea among some people at the time that fairies were the souls of the dead that remained on earth. Indeed looking at accounts of hauntings from the 16th to 18th centuries it is notable that ghosts, fairies, angels, and demons exhibit extremely similar characteristics. It was usually only the context in which they appeared that allowed them to be identified as one or the other.

There have been a number of reasons put forward for why the spirits of the dead would want to haunt the living. Before the Reformation in England (during the reign of Henry VIII, 1509–1547) many ghosts returned to request masses to be said for their souls, bemoaning the fact that they could not otherwise enter heaven. In later centuries, someone might come back as a ghost, because their personal affairs had been left in confusion when they died. Legal injustices were another reason for the dead to return. Perhaps the most dramatic motif for a haunting was that of revenge, the ghost often taking the form of the victim of a murder seeking retribution from their killer. Other hauntings were said to be caused by those whose life had been so wicked that they were condemned to wander the earth as lost, imprisoned spirits. Other common candidates for a return from the grave were those who had died tragically, especially suicides. Some ghosts could not rest because their remains had not been buried with the correct rites (a particularly common motif in classical tales), others due to the disturbance of their graves by some unfeeling mortal. A number of ghosts, though, were far less sensational, returning merely to continue the routine they had enjoyed on earth, perhaps visiting a favorite place or pursuing their former place of employment as if they had never left.

It is impossible to separate the reasons for and functions of ghostly visitors from the purpose and motives of those who have recorded apparitions and hauntings through the years. Any examination of stories of hauntings from the ancient world up until the present will reveal how the reports are manipulated to reflect contemporary events and concerns. Indeed, it would be true to say that every era experiences its ghosts according to a defined set of traditions and expectations, most frequently based on religious doctrines regarding the afterlife and social conventions. There were a number of important studies of hauntings made in the 17th century, which still exert an influence on the way we see, research, and record ghosts today. Probably the most significant of these was Joseph Glanvill's *Saducismus Triumphatus* (1681). In this book, Glanvill, a clergyman and philosopher who believed in the malign power of witches and magic, advocated the investigation and examination of supernatural occurrences in order to prove their existence. Glanvill vehemently attacked those skeptical of demonic powers and maintained that the denial of such spirits and demons was tantamount to atheism. Other writers of the same period, including English Puritan church leader and theologian Richard Baxter (1615–1691) and Richard Bovet, author of *Pandaemonium, or the Devil''s Cloyster* (1684), recorded accounts of hauntings and witchcraft with the express purpose of demonstrating and maintaining a religious system where ghosts and angels revealed the hand of God in human affairs, while witches and demons were proof of the very real existence and influence of the Devil, the arch enemy of the Christian faith.

Similarly the rise of spiritualism in the mid to late 19th century reflected the desire of many people for proof of an afterlife. In the more materialistic Victorian society, people naturally required tangible proof of spirits, rather than mere tales, hence the appearance of the darkened séance rooms and such things as "spirit photographs," "ectoplasm," and scientific experiments into alleged spirit manifestations.

Nowadays, there are myriad reasons why a ghost is thought to appear and why such stories are recorded. The media, especially the Internet, has a huge role in collecting, exaggerating, and disseminating ghostly tales of varying degrees of reliability. Local books on ghosts and the supernatural are hugely popular, though similar works about regional folklore are much less well known, which is surprising, because many of them contain the same tales, though told in a less sensational manner. "ghost tours" and ghost walks," as well as "haunted" pubs, have become a significant part of the tourist industry, both in the United Kingdom and in the United States. Though, as Owen Davies notes, in the classic work on the English pub, Thomas Burke's *The English Inn* (1930), there are only a few stories of ghosts, though plenty about murders, highwaymen, and the visits of various kings and queens.

But do ghosts exist? Those skeptical of ghosts and the paranormal in general object, on many levels, to the reality of the numerous hauntings and apparitions recorded through the centuries. They point out that secondhand anecdotal evidence is not scientific proof of the existence of spirits of the dead or any other kind of phantom. Rather than indicating the existence of an afterlife or a fourth dimension, skeptics argue that all tales of ghosts can be explained by errors in human perception and misunderstood ordinary natural phenomena. Although these explanations may very well be true for the majority of sightings, the ghost is such a complicated phenomenon that one or two relatively simplistic explanations cannot hope to account for the whole range of variations within the subject. But whether ghosts exist only in the minds of those who report them is a question I will leave my readers to decide. *The Lore of the Ghost* is not a book about ghost hunting or a gazetteer of ghost sightings; there are plenty of those works already. It is rather an investigation into human belief in the supernatural and its affect on how ghosts are interpreted and recorded. Ghost stories are certainly "true" in the sense that they give us an important insight into the major concerns, the traditions, and the psychology of the individuals and the societies in which they circulate. This alone makes them a vital and constantly developing aspect of popular belief.

Chapter 1

The Wild Hunt

The Wild Hunt is the generic term for the apparition of a huntsman or group of huntsmen riding black horses and usually accompanied by a pack of phantom hounds. The Hunt was more often heard rather than seen, thundering across the sky at night over the forests and woods of Northern and Western Europe in the manner of a violent storm. The Hunters in this spectral parade were usually identified as the dead or sometimes as fairies. The "Fairy Rade" of Ireland and Lowland Scotland, a solemn mounted procession of fairy nobility, is a version of the Wild Hunt motif. Toward the end of the Middle Ages, in England, the Hunt began to be associated with witchcraft—the potent image of a host of screaming witches led by a

demon or perhaps even Satan himself was often used by min-
isters to frighten congregations.

Throughout its long history, the myth/folk motif of the Wild
Hunt has constantly been modified, with various local and na-
tional gods and folk heroes taking on the role as its leader. In
Scandinavian countries, it was usually Odin or, in Denmark,
Valdemar Atterdag (usually called "King Waldemar" in English);
in Germany, Woden (Odin) and Hackelnberg; in Wales, Gwynn
Ap Nudd, King of the Fairies; and in England, Herne the
Hunter, King Herla, and even Elizabethan explorer Sir Francis
Drake. The fact that the Wild Hunt could be led by the Devil is
in keeping with one of the Huntsman's roles as a demonic figure collecting the souls of sinners. The Wild Hunt was known
by various names throughout Europe, including the Mesnee
d'Hellequin in Northern France, Herlathing (England),
Cwn Annwn (Wales), Woden's Hunt and the Raging Host
in Germany, the Oskorei in Norway, Odensjakt in Denmark
and Sweden, and Ghost Riders—a group of phantom cowboys
doomed to ride the sky forever in pursuit of the Devil's herd—
in the United States. Wherever it appeared, the Hunt was an
ominous sign portending death or disaster, and is thus closely
connected in folklore and myth with the Black Dog, the Headless
Horseman, and the Death Coach (see the respective chapters
in this book). Indeed the English folk motif of the "hell waine"
("hell wagon"), a death coach known in Ireland as the "coach-
a-bower," performs a similar function to the Wild Hunt roar-
ing around the country at night collecting the souls of the
damned. Most reports of so-called "phantom coaches" during
the last 200 years or so have their origin in tales of the Wild
Hunt.

The Wild Hunt

The ancient origin of the folk motif of the Wild Hunt is difficult to trace, though it is undoubtedly, as described by Ari Berk and William Spytma in their article "Penance, Power, and Pursuit: On the Trail of the Wild Hunt," "an embodiment of the memories of war, agricultural myth, ancestral worship, and royal pastime." In Norway, Sweden, and Denmark the name *Odensjakt* means "Odin's Hunt," and it is in Odin (Teutonic—"Woden") the chief divinity of the Norse pantheon, that many characteristics of the Wild Huntsman may be found. In his role as a wind god, Odin would blast through the sky riding his magical eight-legged horse, Sleipnir, gathering the souls of the dead. The arrival of Odin's Hunt was signaled by the baying of hounds, the hoof beats of horses, roars of thunder, crashes of lightning, and furious winds. Odin, charging across the night sky followed by the ghosts of the dead, would presage catastrophes such as war, plague, and the death of all who witnessed the terrifying scene.

As Susan Hilary Houston notes in her article "Ghost Riders in the Sky," in *Western Folklore* (July 1964), there may be a further connection between the Wild Hunt and the saga of Odin, in the wild rides of the Valkyries (Old Norse *Valkyrja* "Choosers of the Slain"). These minor female deities were Odin's handmaidens, and soared over battlefields mounted upon winged horses and armed with helmets and spears, ready to carry off the slain to Valhalla. The role of the Valkyries as collectors of the souls of dead warriors ties in well with the primary function of Odin's Wild Hunt, though Houston's contention that the Valkyries were "the original Wild Hunters" is perhaps stretching the evidence too much.

It is from England that the first description of an unearthly procession of the dead is described as a hunt, recorded in the *Peterborough Chronicle* for the year of 1127:

Lore of the Ghost

Let it not be thought remarkable, when we tell the truth, because it was fully known over all the country, that as soon as he came there...then soon afterwards many people saw and heard many hunters hunting. The hunters were black and big and loathsome, and their hounds all black and wide-eyed and loathsome, and they rode on black horses and black goats. This was seen in the very deer-park in the town of Peterborough, and in all the woods that there were between his town and Stamford, and the monks heard the horns blow that they were blowing at night. Trustworthy people noticed them at night, and said that it seemed to them there might well be about twenty or thirty hornblowers. This was seen and heard from the time he came there all Lent up to Easter.

This terrifying description of the Wild Hunt from Peterborough Abbey was written by monks as a portent for the coming of Henry of Poitou, a greedy and scheming abbot appointed to the post, in their opinion, only because he was related to King Henry I. Writing later in the same century, around 1190, Walter Map in his *De Nugis Curialium* ("Courtier's Trifles") talks of King Herla, a legendary king of the ancient Britons who became the leader of the Wild Hunt after a visit to the Otherworld. Map, an English author of Welsh descent, describes "nocturnal companies" known as the "familia Herletbingi"—the "household of Herlethingus."

In English folklore, as in that of other countries, when the original name and meaning of the Wild Hunt had begun to fade from memory, the command of the Hunt was increasingly inferred upon various well known leaders from the past. As in

Germany, in England the Hunt could be led by a historical or semi-historical figure, as well as a completely fictional one. One historical example was Eadric the Wild, a leader of English Saxon resistance to the 11th century Norman Conquest, who held extensive lands in Shropshire and Herefordshire, in the English Midlands. Legends associate Eadric with the Wild Hunt, and say that Eadric still lies sleeping under the Shropshire hills and, similar to King Arthur, will return to lead the Hunt in a phantom procession across the sky whenever England is in danger. On the eve of the Crimean War in 1853 or 1854, a young woman from the village of Rorrington, in west Shropshire, claimed to have heard the sound of a horn and witnessed the Wild Hunt led by Wild Eadric riding a white horse. She described Eadric as having short dark hair, a green cap with a white feather in it, a short green coat and a cloak, and a horn and sword hanging from his golden belt. He was accompanied by his wife Lady Godda, queen of the faeries, who had golden hair flowing to her waist, a band of white linen containing a gold ornament around her head, a green dress, and a short dagger at her waist.

Another leader of the Hunt in English folklore and mythology was Herne the Hunter. Though Herne is believed by some to be a real person, perhaps a gamekeeper who worked in King Richard II's (1377–1399) estate of Windsor Forest, Berkshire, it is more likely that the Herne figure represents the wildness of the forest itself. In *The Merry Wives of Windsor*, first published in 1602, Shakespeare has Falstaff impersonate Herne:

There is an old tale goes that Herne the Hunter,
Sometime a keeper here in Windsor Forest,
Doth all the winter-time, at still midnight,
Walk round about an oak, with great ragg'd horns;

Lore of the Ghost

And there he blasts the tree, and takes the cattle,
And makes milch-kine yield blood, and shakes a chain
In a most hideous and dreadful manner.
You have heard of such a spirit, and well you know ^
The superstitious idle-headed eld
Receiv'd, and did deliver to our age,
This tale of Herne the Hunter for a truth
(Shakespeare, *The Merry Wives of Windsor*, 4.4.28–38)

In the Parish of St. Germans, Cornwall, in the south west of England, the version of the Wild Hunt legend is known as Dando and his Dogs or the Dandy Dogs. The story involved the Devil carrying off a dissolute priest named Dando who went hunting on Sundays. Since then, he and his dogs are seen or heard galloping across the moorland and valleys on dark nights. In Wales and the west of England, the leader of the Hunt was said to be Gwynn ap Nudd. As the King of the Welsh fairies (the "Tylwyth Teg") and the Lord of the Dead, Gwynn ap Nudd drives the Cwn Annwn (the "Hounds of the Otherworld," sometimes called the Hounds of Hell), his pack of white hounds with blood-red ears in the pursuit of the souls of the recently deceased. In the North of England, this spectral group of hounds with red ears was known as the Gabriel Hounds. These supernatural beasts were said to foretell death by their yelping at night, and were once believed to be the souls of unbaptized children wandering around the skies waiting for Judgement Day.

English statesman and writer Gervase of Tilbury, writing around 1212 in the *Otia imperialia* ("Recreation for an Emperor") calls the Hunt *familia Arturi*, "the household of Arthur," and later, in the early 13th century in some parts of France, it was known as *la Chasse Artus* ("Arthur's Hunt"). In England, there are tales of King Arthur and his men thundering by on moon-lit winter nights at Castle-An-Dinas, Cornwall, and also at South Cadbury hillfort, Somerset, both ancient sites associ-ated with a possibly historical King Arthur. Harlequin, the masked character of Early Modern theatre, is also associated with the Wild Hunt. Probably a version of King Herla, the ori-gin of Harlequin seems to lie in *Hellequin*, a black-faced mes-senger of the devil in the Medieval French miracle plays. Hellequin was said to originate inside of the earth, hence his blackened face, and would roam the countryside at night with a group of demonic horsemen, known as *la Maisnie Hellequin* ("Hellequin's Escort"), pursuing the damned souls of evil people to Hell.

In Germany, there were two aspects to the Wild Hunt myth, the *Wilde Jagd* ("Wild Hunt") of Northern Germany and the *Wutendes Heer* ("Furious Host") of the south. However, the two are not identical. Although it was the function of the *Wutendes Heer* to warn of future catastrophes, the *Wilde Jagd* was the more feared, as it could cause immediate disaster. The German Wild Hunt would appear sometimes as a warlike troop, or on other occasions as a band of hunters. In some parts of Germany, the *Wilde Jagd* could even be led by female deities, such as Perchta, Holda, and Frau Gauden, who would lead a train of unbaptized children through the night sky. Such pagan soul-gatherers soon became demonized by the Church in the Middle Ages and consequently it was soon the Devil himself who was said to lead the Wild Hunt.

The Brothers Grimm collected a number of tales of the German Wild Hunt in the early 19th century, the most accessible col-lection of their stories in English being *The German Legends of the Brothers Grimm* (1981) edited by Donald Ward. By the time the brothers were recording German folktales the leader of the Hunt was generally believed to be Hans von Hackelnberg (said to have died in either 1521 or 1581), the semi-historical chief huntsman to the duke of Brunswick in Lower Saxony, northwestern Germany. The tale "Hackelnberg, The Wild Huntsman" tells how the huntsman was so dedicated to the chase that when he lay on his deathbed he prayed to God that he could exchange his place in Heaven for permission to follow the hunt in Solling Forest "until Judgement Day." The irreverent huntsman also asked to be buried in Solling Forest. As a result of this agreement, four times every night the terrible echoing sounds of the hunting horn can be heard "signaling the chase and the baying of the hounds can be heard in the wilderness." It was also believed that if anyone heard the sounds of the Hunt during the night, but persisted in going hunting the following day, he would suffer terrible misfortune or receive a serious injury during the chase, possibly even a broken neck.

The narrator of the story of Hackelnberg, Hans Kirchhof of Wendunmuth, relates an experience he claimed to have had while riding through Solling Forest on the way from the town of Einbech to Ublar in southern Lower Saxony:

> I became lost and chanced upon Hackelnberg's grave. It was located in a clearing something like a meadow, but it was covered with a wild growth and with reeds. It measured about an acre and was somewhat longer than it was wide. Though the area was surrounded by trees, none grew on this clearing. One end extended toward sunrise, and at the other end there was a raised, flat red stone about eight or nine feet long, and about— as it seemed to me—five feet wide. The stone did

not face toward the east as gravestones usually do, but instead one end pointed south and the other north. I was told than no one would ever be able to find this grave—whether from inquisitiveness or from a sense of purpose—no matter how determined and adventurous he might be. But if someone should chance upon the site, he would find a pack of frightful black dogs next to it. I, however, saw no such spooky apparition...

In another tale of Grimm's tales of Hackelnberg, "Toot Osel," the Wild Huntsman is recorded as being witnessed at midnight in his carriage with his yelping hounds leading the way, "rushing through storm and rain." In this particular story, a night owl flies before him, called by the local people Toot Osel. Any travelers who encountered this ghostly owl would throw themselves to the ground face down and let the Wild Hunt pass by above them, with the phantom pack of hounds barking furiously and the Huntsman calling out "Hoho! Hoho!" Similarly, in tales of the Raging Horde from Upper and Middle Germany, an old man known as "Faithful Eckhart" went before the host carrying a white staff and warning people to clear the way as harm would befall them if they witnessed the ghostly procession.

Two other stories from the Grimms illustrate another motif of the Wild Hunt legend, found also in England, that describes the punishment of a mortal who mocks the hunt in some way. In "The Wild Huntsman and the Tailor" a tailor sitting at his work bench next to a window heard the furious noise of the Wild Hunt passing overhead and cried out mockingly, "Hoho! Hoho! Kliffklaff, kliffklaff!" Suddenly a horse's hoof crashed through the window and struck the tailor such a blow

that he fell to the floor almost dead. When he managed to re-
gain consciousness he heard a terrible voice shouting, "If thou
wouldst hunt with me, then thou wilt suffer with me!" In the
Grimms' "The Wild Huntsman Pursues the Moss People," the
Moss People—"little men and women who lie upon green moss
and are clothed all over in green moss," are described as being
the sport of the Wild Huntsman. On one occasion, a peasant
from Arntschgereute, near Saalfeld, (east-central Germany)
was cutting trees in the mountains when he heard the terrible
din of the Wild Hunt approaching. Wanting to join in the Hunt
the peasant began yelling like a hunter, but the hunt passed by
and the man finished his work and went home. The next morning, when the peasant entered his stable, he found a quarter of
a Moss Woman hanging there "as though she was his share of
the catch." A local nobleman, Lord von Watzdorf, later told
the terrified man not to touch the body as the Huntsman would
challenge him for it. The peasant followed his advice and the
game soon vanished from his barn. He never again encountered the Wild Huntsman.

A very similar story, from Wistman's Wood in Dartmoor,
Devon, in the southwest of England, is recounted by the Rev.
Sabine Baring-Gould in *A Book of the West* (1899). This wood
was allegedly haunted by one of England's many packs of spectral hounds, in Devon known as the Wish (or Wisht) Hounds.
One night a farmer was riding home from Widdecombe Fair
passing an ancient stone alignment when a pack of phantom
hounds led by a ghostly huntsman flew silently and swiftly by
him. Seemingly undaunted the plucky farmer called out to the
huntsman asking him for a share of his game. "Take that!"
replied the huntsman, flinging down a bundle as he passed
overhead. As it was dark the farmer waited until he arrived

home to find out what was inside the mysterious bundle, but when he opened it he was horrified to discover that it contained the body of his own child.

Chapter 2

Phantom White Ladies

The tradition of the ghostly woman in white, a class of ghost so called because of the white color of her dress, is found in a number of different countries, though the majority of examples quoted in this chapter come from Britain and Germany. This particular ghostly motif can have a number of different functions, depending on the context and the culture in which it is recorded. In the folklore of Britain, phantom white ladies are often associated with pools, wells, and rivers, while in Germany she is sometimes reported as carrying keys or as a half human "Snake Maiden." The association of ghostly white ladies with ruined castles and treasure is also a frequently occurring motif in most of the countries where she is said to appear. Another common role of the white lady is that of a murdered woman returning from the dead seeking justice or revenge for her untimely fate.

As has been stated previously, the white ladies of Britain are often associated with water, and one of the best known of these white lady hauntings is from Longnor in Shropshire. The Black Pool at Longnor was said to be bottomless and inhabited by a white lady who would come out and dance on the green at night. In her classic work, *Shropshire Folk-Lore* (1883), Charlotte Sophia Burne relates the story of a servant of the local parish priest named Hughes who encountered the Longnor woman in white in June 1881. Crossing the footbridge over Longnor Brook, Hughes saw what he presumed to be a local girl walking toward him and tried to scare her by grabbing her as she passed by, but when he clasped his arms around the girl she vanished. Hughes also told Charlotte Burne that the white lady of Longnor had once attended a village dance and joined in with the locals dancing around in a ring. Although no one suspected anything unusual people did notice that the girl's neighbors in the dance were never able to take hold of her hand. After a while the girl disappeared from the dance and the villagers soon discovered that it had been the white lady among them. The locals' explanation for the phantom white lady was that she was the ghost of a woman who had drowned herself in the Black Pool. Charlotte Burne notes the interesting fact in relation to this story that the term *white lady* had been used in the area of Longnor to describe fairies since the 11th century. The dancing around in a circle too, Burne also notes, indicates the fairy origins of the Longnor Pool white lady.

Two more instances where a ghostly white lady is connected with water come from the county of Yorkshire, in the north of England. The first is quoted in Jane Beck's article "The White Lady of Great Britain and Ireland" in *Folklore*, winter, 1970:

> At that point where the Hodge and the Dove mix their waters is to be seen on Hallowe'en a lovely maiden robed in white and having long golden hair down about her waist there standing with her bare

arm thrown about her companion's neck which is a
lovely white doe but she alloweth none to come near
unto her.

The other Yorkshire case comes from W. Hylton Dyer Longstaffe's
History and Antiquities of the Parish of Darlington (1854). The name
of a stream haunted by the white lady, "White-lass-beck," derived
from the spectral visitor who had the unusual though not unique
ability to shape shift, "turning into a white dog and an ugly animal,"
according to Longstaffe. As is frequently the case with white ladies,
the local explanation for the haunting was that, some time previously, a local girl had been murdered, and when a skeleton was discovered in a gravel pit near the stream a few years later it was
thought to be that of the unfortunate girl.

A certain young man near Carmarthen, in south west Wales, often observed a group of shape-shifting white ladies at night crossing
the River Towy and vanishing mysteriously when they arrived at the
other side. On one occasion the man hid himself behind some bushes
in the hope of getting to the bottom of the mystery. He watched the
strange ladies carefully, and when they were in mid-stream the light
of the moon revealed that they were sailing in cockle-shells, and when
they arrived at the opposite bank of the river they vanished and black
cats appeared. Apparently, these ladies were the white witches of
Carmarthen, who had the ability to transform themselves into cats.

Another example of the ghostly white lady's association with
wells, streams, and rivers comes from the neighborhood of the
magnificent 17th-century Ragley Hall, in Warwickshire, in the English Midlands. According to J. Harvey Bloom writing in *Folk Lore,
Old Customs and Superstitions in Shakespeare Land* (1930) a white
lady would appear at midnight and sit upon a stile close to the
hall, and then go down to a nearby brook to drink. In their book,
Midland Spirits and Spectres (1998), Anne Bradford and Barrie
Roberts note some more appearances of this particular white lady

apparition in connection with a spring in the area, mostly dating to the first half of the 20th century. On one occasion in 1912, the phantom was seen at 11 p.m. by a group of 10 young local girls who, as quoted by Bradford and Roberts, described her as a "misty white lady floating across the road from left to right." A more recent sighting noted by the authors occurred in the 1990s, and was reported by a lady named Anne Cooke. The case is described as follows in *Midland Spirits and Spectres*:

> We live in Redditch but both work shifts in Exall, so that we drive along the A435 nearly every day and at all times. My husband had been on his way home at about 10:40 in the evening when his headlights picked out a white shape in the trees just by the Springs. As he drew nearer he looked more carefully and saw that it was a young lady wearing a white dress, crouching high up on a branch of the tree. Suddenly, to his horror, the young lady jumped off the tree and was left hanging by her neck. It was a grisly scene and it really shook him. He slowed down and looked back but the woman and the tree had disappeared.

Some time in 1833, the skeleton of an Anglo-Saxon woman, accompanied by brooches and a dagger was discovered in the area around Ragley and there was speculation linking the ancient find with the White Lady tradition here. Unfortunately, as we do not know whether the origins of this phantom lady tale predate the discovery of the body it is impossible to know whether local folklore has somehow retained a dim tradition of an actual person or event. What is certain is that in this case the white lady of the springs, with her appearance on a stile and near water (both liminal places), possesses two typical characteristics of ghost lore.

There are a surprising number of tales in the annals of folklore connecting white ladies with castles, treasure, and mysterious secrets.

Hadleigh Castle, overlooking the River Thames in Essex, south east England, was begun around 1231 and substantially enlarged in the mid-14th century. Philip Benton, writing in his *History of Rochford Hundred* (1867), mentions an old lady who related a tradition of a woman in white who once haunted the castle ruins. The tale concerns a milkmaid who lived at the castle farm, and met the woman in white in the castle precincts one morning at sunrise. The apparition told the girl to meet her again in the same place at midnight when she would reveal mysteries connected with the castle. But the girl was so afraid that she did not keep the appointment. Early the next morning she encountered the woman in white again, who reproached her bitterly for not doing as she was commanded and gave her a violent slap on the ear for her trouble. The poor milkmaid never recovered fully from this vicious blow and from that time onward ahe was always known as "wry-neck Sall."

A similar tale is connected with 14th-century Blenkinsopp Castle, in Northumberland, in the North East of England. Some time in the late 1700s (or early 1800s, accounts vary) the parents of an 8-year-old boy were woken up in the middle of the night by his screaming. When the parents calmed their son down he told them that a finely dressed white lady had appeared in the room and sat on his bed, but had become angry at him when he would not follow her. The lady had told the boy that she would make him a rich man, as many hundreds of years previously she had hidden a large chest of gold down in the castle vaults. If he helped her recover the treasure she would give it to him. As the lady was lifting the boy up to take him with her, however, he cried out and frightened her away.

In Welsh folklore, the white lady ("Ladi Wen") is often connected with treasure, though she often has a more sinister nature than the female specter of English tales. Ogmore Castle, in the Ewenny estuary near the town of Bridgend, South Wales, was built by the

Normans soon after 1100, and has a particularly interesting white lady tale connected with it. This phantom, recorded by Marie Trevelyan in *Folk-lore and Folk-Stories of Wales* (1909), was traditionally supposed to guard a treasure kept under the floor of the castle tower. During one of her appearances a man had the courage to speak to her, after which the lady took him to the spot where the treasure was concealed and asked him to lift a large flag stone. On moving the stone, he found a hole dug underneath, inside of which was an old earthenware jar full of golden guineas. The mysterious lady told the man to take half of the treasure and leave the rest for her, which he did, and replaced the heavy stone. Some time later, the man became greedy and returned to the spot, lifted the stone, and filled his pockets with the rest of the treasure. But just as he was making his departure the white lady appeared and accused him of stealing the coins. This he denied, but when the lady told him to take off his coat the gold clattered to the floor. At this the white lady attacked him with her sharp claws, which she possessed instead of fingers, and he only barely escaped with his life. Not long after this incident the man fell mysteriously ill and was very soon on the verge of death. Before he passed away the unfortunate man confessed to his family and friends what had happened with the treasure and the white lady of Ogmore Castle. According to Marie Trevelyan local people called his complaint "the white lady's revenge."

Only a few miles from Ogmore Castle, between the village of Ewenny and Bridgend, close to the 12th-century Ewenny Priory, are places named White Lady's Meadow and White Lady's Lane. According to Trevelyan it was once a tradition in the area that a white lady would appear and point in the direction of Ewenny, or sometimes she was seen wringing her hands as if in despair. It was thought by some that she knew where treasure was hidden. On one occasion a man spoke to her and she seemed relieved. He wanted to help her and she told him that if he could hold her tightly in both arms until she told him to stop then all her problems would be solved. The man did as the lady asked him, but a dog barking loudly nearby caused him to look a round and release the white lady from his grasp. At this she let out a loud scream and cried out "I shall be bound for another seven years!" A local story links the origin of the white lady to a terrible crime committed in a now demolished house in the meadow at some time in the past. Because of this misdeed the woman's spirit was bound to roam the earth as penance. The Ewenny white lady and the Ogmore Castle example are so similar in detail and so close geographically that it is likely that we have two different versions of the same story.

There are a number of examples of ghostly women in white connected with castles in *The German Legends of the Brothers Grimm*, edited by Donald Ward (1981). In the tale Mother Bertha or the White Woman the lady in white appears walking the halls of the castles of certain royal families, most particularly the residences of Neuhaus in Bohemia, Berlin, Bayreuth, Darmstadt, and Karlruhe. This lady seems like a harmless ghost; when she is encountered she simply bows her head, but her appearance wearing a black glove signifies that death is coming to the castle. Conversely, when she is not wearing a black glove to encounter her can be a good omen. As with many German "Key Maiden" tales, this white lady carries a ring of keys and wears a veiled white hood.

In the Grimms' The Maiden of the Castle a girl in white carrying a large ring of keys is said to appear at Castle Mountain near the small town of Ohrdruf in the German federal state of Thuringia. The lady appears at noon and comes down the mountain to bathe in Horling Springs in the valley below (see the Ragley Hall lady in white for the same characteristic). In The Maiden of Osel Mountain a beautiful maiden lived in a castle that once stood on Osel Mountain, between Dinkelsbühl and Hahnkamm in Bavaria. This girl lived at the castle with her widowed father and as she organized the household for him she held the keys for all the rooms in the building. One day the ancient walls of the castle gave way and collapsed burying the young girl alive. Not long afterward, it was said that the ghost of the unfortunate girl could be seen during the four fasting periods called Ember Days, floating around the ruined castle carrying a ring of keys. It was also rumored that on some occasions this phantom girl could be seen in the shape of a large serpent, with a woman's head and breasts.

Ladies in white who wander forlornly through ancient ruined castles are also found in central European folklore. At least three are known from Slovakia, one from Bratislava Old Town, another from Bojnice castle, and the last from the medieval town of Levoča, in the Spiš region of eastern Slovakia. The origin of this latter white lady is said to be a woman named Júlia Korponayová, who came from the village of Ožiany, near Rimavská Sobota in southern Slovakia. Korponayová was arrested after being caught spying for the Hapsburg emperor and was executed on September 25, 1714, in the Hungarian town of Győr.

Tales of ghostly women in white are not confined to Europe. The journal *Western Folklore*, for April 1947, quoted a story from the *Rocky Mountain News* from October 7, 1946. The incident came from the southern Colorado town of Aguilar, where it was reported that an 18-year-old boy had been seized from behind by a phantom lady at midnight and scared out of his wits. The ghost was also seen beside the churchyard, and was described by one old resident of the town, as quoted by the *Rocky Mountain News*, as "a woman, wearing a long dress, all in white. She walks around the churchyard at night. She cries like a baby. She's unhappy about something, but I don't know what. I saw her walking there, but she vanished into thin air."

Often reported as a gliding specter, the white lady has been interpreted simply as a ghost wearing the white clothes of the grave, or wrapped in a white shroud. However, if this is the case it remains a puzzle why there are so few reports of ghostly men in white. One popular theory for the origin of phantom white ladies is that they were originally female divinities degraded through time to become ghosts, though the notion that the white lady is the last vestiges of some hypothetical mother goddess cult is entirely without foundation. However, in one or two cases there may be some truth to the idea that this particular class of ghost is related to a once great goddess. In some of the Grimm's' German tales, the resemblance between the white ladies and the Teutonic goddess Frau Holda or Holle and her sacred pool through which the souls of newborn babies entered the world, is obvious. It is also possible that the association of white ladies with sacred wells and pools may indicate an origin for a few of these spectres in the Christian saints associated with such bodies of water, or perhaps even the pre-Christian pagan deities connected with the same places. However, the chance that the memory of such ancient divinities survived for 1,500 years or more is slight.

The most important aspect of ghostly white ladies is their association with wells, pools, rivers, fords, bridges, stiles, gates, and other liminal places. This characteristic, a common motif in ghost lore, is extremely significant as it was at such places, the boundaries between the known and the unknown, between life and death, that supernatural entities were expected to appear. The many examples of the White Lady place name in England and Wales, often with no explanatory history or tale attached, perhaps indicates a fairy association rather than a ghostly one. As Owen Davies notes in *The Haunted: A Social History of Ghosts* (2007), tales of phantom ladies in white appear at roughly the same time, the 18th century, that fairy beliefs were dying out. Perhaps many of the tales of white ladies in Britain were originally traditions of fairy women, reinterpreted as ghosts to suit the times.

Chapter 3

Spectral Armies and Battles

There is a long tradition from a variety of different cultures of stories of phantom battles in the sky and marching ghostly armies appearing in front of bewildered witnesses. These apparitions are predominantly seen or heard at the site of former, or even future, battle sites. The Bible contains a number of examples of spectral armies helping the Israelites in times of need, and such phantoms are also described as being witnessed during the Maccabee Wars (from 169 to 166 BC) in ancient Judaea, and before the fall of Jerusalem to Titus in AD 70. A well, known account of a spectral battle is featured in the *Description of Greece*, written in the 2nd century AD by Greek geographer and travel writer Pausanias. While describing the villagers living near the plain of Marathon, north of Athens, where the Athenians had defeated the Persians in

490 BC, Pausanias states "here every night you can hear the noise of whinnying horses and of men fighting." Though the Greek writer does not mention if anything was actually seen, this brief description is a blueprint for stories of ghostly armies haunting battlefields, which were to appear through the centuries.

In *The City of God* St. Augustine (AD 354–430) discusses the case of a phantom battle between "evil spirits" on a plain in Campania, southern Italy:

> These evil spirits...were seen in a wide plain in Campania rehearsing among themselves the battle which shortly after took place there with great bloodshed between the armies of Rome...at first there were heard loud crashing noises, and afterwards many reported that they had seen for some days together two armies engaged. And when this battle ceased, they found the ground all indented with just such footprints of men and horses as a great conflict would leave.

This report is notable for the fact that the spectral battle actually fulfills the function of an omen, as the battle depicted by the spirits had not yet taken place. During the medieval period in Europe, the ghostly battle, along with the majority of other types of apparitions, was given a religious interpretation. A particularly singular account is mentioned in R.C. Finucane's authoritative *Appearances of the Dead, A Cultural History of Ghosts* (1982). The report dates from the 12th century and involves the apparition of a Spanish soldier named Sancho who had fought for Alphonso II (1152–1196), at Castile. The soldier had been dead four months when his ghost appeared naked "except for a slight covering upon his shameful parts," to his old lord one night while the latter was in bed. Sancho informed his former master that he was on his way to Castile with a vast army of the dead to perform penance for sins committed there. The Specter also claimed that his lord's wife had an unpaid debt to him, which he now asked to be donated to the poor. After further questions Sancho was summoned back to the ghostly army by another dead soldier, was who also naked and who stood at the window, before both apparitions vanished. Apart from the need to make amends for war crimes, the function of this slightly bizarre tale is linked to another extremely common motif in medieval tales of the returning dead, that of the request for prayers, psalms, and masses to ease the sufferings of purgatory.

The first battle of the English Civil War took place at Edgehill in Warwickshire on October 23, 1642. Three months after the bloody encounter, in January 1643, a pamphlet appeared entitled *A Great Wonder in Heaven*, which described how on a series of weekends around the previous Christmas there had occurred the apparition and noise of a battle in the air, a ghostly repetition of the conflict which, two months before, had taken place on the adjacent fields at Edgehill between the forces of the King and the Parliament.

Though the outcome of the actual battle of Edgehill was inconclusive, in the visions the Royalists were defeated. Reports of the phantom battle eventually reached King Charles, then staying at Oxford, who sent six trustworthy emissaries to investigate. According to the pamphlet, these six gentlemen also witnessed the phenomenon, and even recognized several of the slain soldiers. The pamphlet concludes by stating:

> What this doth portend, God only Knoweth, and Time will perhaps discover; but doubtlessly it is a sign of His wrath against this land for these civil wars, which may He in His good time finish, and send a sudden peace between his Majestie and Parliament.

A number of pamphlets were published during the Civil War spouting propaganda for both the Crown and Parliament, and though the Edge Hill account supports neither side, it can be viewed as a general warning about Divine punishment for wrongdoing, much in the same vein as accounts of apparitions during the medieval period were utilized for religious purposes. As the pamphlet seems to be the origin of the Edgehill phantom battle, later sightings of spectral armies in the area must be viewed with some suspicion. Since the 17th century there have been one or two reports by local inhabitants who have claimed to hear what they thought were the noises of fighting armies, usually around the time of the anniversary of the battle, and there have also been occasional sightings of individual ghosts on horseback thought to be connected with the conflict. Similar stories of ghostly battalions were told after another Civil War battle at Naseby in Northamptonshire, fought on June 14, 1645.

An intriguing phantom army story from Souther Fell, in the Lake District, Cumberland, northwest England, was published in the *Gentleman's Magazine* in 1747:

> On Midsummer-eve, 1735, Wm. Lancaster's servant related that he saw the east side of Souter-Fell, towards the top, covered with a regular marching army for above an hour together; he said they consisted of distinct bodies of troops, which appeared to proceed from an eminence in the north end, and marched over a nitch in the top, but, as no other person in the neighbourhood had seen the like, he was discredited and laughed at. Two years after, on Midsummer-eve also, betwixt the hours of eight and nine, Wm Lancaster himself imagined that several gentlemen were following their horses at a distance, as if they had been hunting...about ten minutes

after...they appeared to be mounted, and a vast army following, five in rank, crowding over at the same place, where the servant said he saw them two years before.

The phenomenon was not witnessed again for another decade, on the Midsummer Eve before the Scottish Rebellion of 1745. On this occasion about 26 people witnessed the spectacle, some being so convinced it was a real army that they climbed the mountainside the following morning in search of hoof prints, which they never found. William Lancaster himself never believed what he saw could have been a real army due to the difficulty of the terrain and the vast number of troops witnessed. Some years later local villagers believed the apparition to have been a sign of the coming Rebellion. One popular explanation is that the ghostly army of Souther Fell was caused by an optical illusion, and indeed the Lake District is known for producing mirages caused by reflection. Though some may wonder how such a mirage produced a ghostly army, such a supernatural interpretation by the witnesses has a long tradition behind it and connects phantom marching armies and spectral battles to tales of the Wild Hunt. Indeed, when William Lancaster first saw the apparition on Souther Fell he thought the men appeared "as if they had been hunting."

The fierce battles of America's Civil War, which lasted from 1861 to 1865, have produced a number of phantom battle stories. The most haunted battlefield of the campaign would appear to be the site of the Battle of Gettysburg, which took place in the town Gettysburg, Pennsylvania, from July 1 to July 3, 1863. As is par for the course with the phantom battle motif witnesses have reported the sounds of marching armies, gunfire, shouting, and the screams of pain of the dying. Some have even claimed to have seen the bodies of dead soldiers littering the battlefield. A large granite

formation known as "Devil's Den" was the site of particularly ferocious fighting at the Battle of Gettysburg and has gained a reputation through the years as a particularly haunted spot. In this
location and several others around the battlefield, tourists have
reported that their cameras have mysteriously malfunctioned and
have often attributed this to the influence of the spectres of the
Civil War slain. Various buildings in the town of Gettysburg have
their own tales of hauntings, the saddest of which is perhaps the
Jennie Wade House and Museum. On the morning of July 3, 1863,
20-year-old Mary Virginia Wade, better known as Ginnie Wade,
was baking bread for Union soldiers in the kitchen of her sister's
house when a confederate sharpshooter's bullet ripped through
the wooden doors and hit her in the back, killing her instantly.
Ginnie Wade is the only documented civilian casualty from the
Battle of Gettysburg, and the ghost of the unfortunate young girl is
said to wander through the rooms of the house. Why the site of the
Battle of Gettysburg in particular should have so many ghostly tales
connected with it is perhaps best explained by the fact that the
battle was the bloodiest of the Civil War, with a staggering 57,225
casualties for both sides during the entire campaign.

Another 19th-century battle from the United States that also
has its fair share of phantoms took place between June 25 and
June 26, 1876, along a ridge above the Little Bighorn River in
Montana. The Battle of the Little Bighorn, also known as Custer's
Last Stand, was fought between a combined force of Lakota, Northern
Cheyenne, and Arapaho warriors and the 7th Cavalry of the United
States Army, led by Lt. Col. George Armstrong Custer. More than
250 soldiers were killed in the battle, including Custer's entire
detachment of 200 men. Ghostly phenomena that have been re-
ported from what is now the Little Bighorn Battlefield National
Monument include charging warriors on horseback, phantom

skirmishes between braves and soldiers, ghostly lights, and the apparition of General Custer himself in the Battlefield Museum.

A particularly controversial 20th century account from the ancient city of York, in northern England, is perhaps one of the best known phantom army stories. The tale involves an 18-year-old apprentice plumber named Harry Martindale, who sometime in 1953 (the details are a little sketchy) was working in the basement of the Treasurer's House, a building dating back to the medieval period and constructed over the site of a Roman road. While Martindale was in the process of installing a heating system, he claimed to have heard the sound of a trumpet or horn and then witnessed Roman soldiers stepping out of a wall and marching across the floor, to disappear through the opposite wall. The soldiers, some of whom were on horseback, wore helmets, and carried round shields, lances, and short swords. Despite being awe struck at the site, Martindale was able to note a few details, including the tired and unkempt appearance of the troops, their red painted round shields, and the fact that they were only visible from the knees up. The latter point has suggested to some paranormal researchers that as the level of the Roman road was below the basement, the soldiers were only partly visible because they were walking on that ancient surface.

Martindale was apparently in bed with shock for two weeks after the strange sighting, and was made fun of when he told his friends, though he has become somewhat of a local celebrity in more recent years and sticks by his story of the spectral Roman legion. Those sceptical of Martindale's story have noted that the incident occurred in the 1950s, when Hollywood "sword and sandals" epic movies were extremely popular, and it was from such movies that the vast majority of the population received their idea of what a Roman soldier looked like. There is a valid point here:

How did Martindale know that what he was seeing was a Roman legion if not from such Hollywood depictions? It is also interesting that Martindale noted that the arrival of the ghostly troops was signalled by a horn or trumpet, as this is often the case with stories of the Wild Hunt. In the tale Hackelburg, the Wild Huntsman included in The German Legends of the Brothers Grimm, "the terrifying echo of the hunting horn" signals the arrival of the ghostly huntsman and his spectral hounds. In the tale Hans Jagendteufel, from the same volume, a woman out gathering acorns in a forest hears the loud blast of a hunting horn, and turns around to see a headless man wearing a long grey coat and sitting on a grey horse.

One point that stands out about many phantom army stories is that, apart from their function as an illustration of the general opinion about those who have died a violent death, they seem to be relatively pointless. One of the various paranormal explanations for the appearance of ghostly armies and battles is that the extreme emotions experienced during battles, such as severe pain, agonizing death, and mental suffering, somehow remain in the atmosphere around the location of the battle, to be replayed under certain circumstances. Though some witnesses believe they have seen a ghostly re-run of the actual battle or even the wandering spirits of the victims, one important element shared by the majority of phantom battle stories is their resemblance to tales of the Wild Hunt. Writing around 1190 in *De nugis curialium* ("Courtiers' Trifles") English author Walter Map describes the "nocturnal companies and squadrons" of the "Herlethingus," named after the mythical King Herla, the leader of the Hunt:

This household of Herlethingus was last seen in the marches of Wales and Hereford in the first year of the reign of Henry II, about noonday: they travelled as we do, with carts and sumpter horses, pack-saddles and panniers, hawks and hounds, and a concourse of men and women...Those who saw them first raised the whole country against them with horns and shouts, and...because they were unable to wring a word from them by addressing them, made ready to extort an answer with their weapons. They, however, rose up into the air and vanished on a sudden.

The similarities between spectral armies and Map's description of the Wild Hunt are obvious, and in European tradition there was a strong connection between the two forms of aerial procession. In northern Europe, the Wild Hunt tradition would seem to be the beginnings of the motif of the spectral host in the sky. It is in keeping with the Wild Hunt tradition that stories of strange phenomena reported from battle sites are interpreted in terms of fighting or marching ghostly armies, whether or not they are caused by optical illusions.

Chapter 4

Ghosts of the Famous

From a quick perusal of the literature devoted to hauntings it is obvious that it is the spirits of famous people, more than any other class of ghost, that have had the habit of returning from beyond the grave to visit the places and people they loved in life. These particularly restless specters include English kings and queens, American presidents, and Hollywood movie stars. But are reports of such illustrious ghosts really more prevalent than those of, for example, run-of-the-mill servant girls or laborers? Or is there some kind of bias either in the reporting of such phantoms or in the expectations and needs of witnesses?

As far as the United Kingdom is concerned, the wives of King Henry VIII (1491–1547) are probably the most frequently reported of royal ghosts. The former royal residence of Hampton

Court Palace, located in the London Borough of Richmond upon Thames, is purportedly haunted by two of Henry VIII's wives. Jane Seymour was Henry's third wife (1507/9–1537). She died of septicemia just 12 days after giving birth to the future King Edward VI of England. The ghost of Jane is said to walk, clad in white and carrying a lighted candle, down the stairs and through the Silver Stick Gallery in the Palace. In stark contrast to Jane's peaceful spirit is the tragic phantom of Katherine Howard. Katherine Howard was Henry's fifth wife, and was beheaded for treason and adultery on Tower Green on February 13, 1542, when still only 21 years of age. Katherine's haunting is a re-enactment of the desperate scene said to have taken place when she was arrested on November 12, 1542. Katherine managed to break away from her guard's clutches and ran through the gallery to the chapel where Henry was at mass, screaming his name and pleading for mercy. Her pleas fell on deaf ears, however, and she was taken by the guards and confined to her rooms in Hampton Court to await execution. The sounds of wild shrieking and the desperate beatings of Katherine's fists against the chapel door were said to echo though the corridors of Hampton Court Palace, until the gallery where this tragic scene took place was reopened in 1918, and the haunting apparently stopped.

Red Lion Square, a small square on the boundary of Bloomsbury, and Holborn, London, is reputedly haunted by three leading Parliamentarians—Oliver Cromwell and his colleagues John Bradshaw and Henry Ireton. The Red Lion Inn, on the Square, is said to be the place where the bodies of the three men were kept overnight before being taken to the gallows at Tyburn to undergo the ritual of "posthumous execution." Cromwell, Lord Protector of England from 1653 to 1658, Bradshaw and Ireton had shared the responsibility for the execution of King Charles I of England on January 30, 1649. After the Restoration of King Charles II in

May 1660, the remains of Cromwell (who had died of natural causes in 1658) and his colleagues were removed from Westminster Abbey, and after the macabre postmortem ritual their heads were placed on poles at Westminster Hall as a warning to others. The ghosts of the three Parliamentarians are said to walk diagonally across Red Lion Square, apparently deep in conversation.

Kensington Palace, a royal residence near Hyde Park, in the Royal Borough of Kensington and Chelsea in London, is the haunt of King George II of England (1683–1760). The German-born king was the last reigning monarch to use the 17th-century Palace. He was confined to the building due to illness and longed to return to his native Hanover, but severe storms prevented any ships from reaching England with news from Germany. King George II died at the Palace on October 25, before the messengers arrived with word from his homeland. The ghost of George II is sometimes seen staring fretfully out of a window of the Palace watching the weathervane above the entrance for a sign that the winds have changed.

In the United States there are a number of stories of hauntings surrounding various presidents of the country. Andrew Jackson, the seventh president of the United States (1829–1837), was heard stomping and cursing around the Rose Room of the White House after his death by Mary Todd Lincoln, the wife of Abraham Lincoln, and a woman with a keen interest in spiritualism. The ghost of Abraham Lincoln himself, U.S. president from 1861–1865, is the most often reported of White House phantoms, perhaps because of his melancholy bearing and the fact that he was the first president of the United States to be assassinated. The first person known to have witnessed Lincoln's ghost was Grace Coolidge (1879–1957), wife of the 30th President Calvin Coolidge. The First Lady apparently saw a tall figure she thought was Lincoln gazing out of the Oval Office window over the Potomac River, as he was wont to do when president. When Queen Wilhelmina of the Netherlands was visiting Franklin and Eleanor Roosevelt at the White House in 1945 she heard a knock on her bedroom door in the dead of night. When she opened the door she found herself face to face with President Lincoln, in a black top hat and traditional dress. Queen Wilhelmina, who also had a prior interest in spiritualism, promptly fainted, and when she recovered, she found herself lying on the floor with the strange figure nowhere to be seen.

Mary Eben, Mrs. Roosevelt's secretary, reported seeing Lincoln's ghost sitting on the bed in the Lincoln bedroom, pulling on his boots as if preparing to go somewhere. Various members of the White House staff during the Roosevelt administration also claimed to have seen Lincoln lying on the bed. Others at the White House in later years, such as Liz Carpenter, press secretary to Lady Bird Johnson, First Lady of the United States from 1963 to 1969, believed they felt Lincoln's presence in various rooms of the building. There is also a legend that Lincoln, like a modern day King Arthur, still watches over his nation, returning to haunt the hall of the second floor of the White House whenever the United States is in danger.

Ghosts associated with show business personalities appear to be particularly active, especially in the United States, though there is one interesting early example from the U.K. British actress Lillie Langtry (1853–1929) led a high-profile and somewhat scandalous life; she was at one time mistress to the Prince of Wales, Queen Victoria's son Albert Edward, the future king Edward VII. Her ghost has been reported from various places including the Edward VII Suite at the luxurious Cadogan Hotel, Sloane Street, London, where Lillie's liaisons with the Prince of Wales took place.

The haunting occurs on Christmas Day when the hotel is quiet. Langtry's ghost, in the form of a Grey Lady, was also seen in the late 1970s at the Langtry Manor Hotel in Bournemouth, on the south coast of England. The hotel, originally called the Red House, was built in 1877 by the Prince of Wales as a home for his mistress.

On Wednesday, August 25, 1926, an estimated 100,000 people lined the streets of New York City to witness the funeral of Italian born actor and romantic idol Rudolph Valentino, who had died of peritonitis two days previously, at the age of 31. Understandably for such a huge and charismatic star, there have been numerous reports of Valentino's spirit. His ghost has been reported from various places throughout southern California, including his beach house in Oxnard, the Santa Maria Inn (where he has been seen reclining on the bed), the costume department at Paramount Studios, and his mansion Falcon Lair, located above Beverly Hills. Valentino's much traveled ghost has also been witnessed near his final resting place in the Cathedral Mausoleum at Hollywood Forever Memorial Park, on Santa Monica Blvd, Hollywood. One of the entrances into Paramount Studios, the Lemon Grove gate, is only a few feet away from the cemetery, and the Italian star has been seen by security guards walking into the studio through this gate.

The original "blonde bombshell," U.S. actress Jean Harlow is said to haunt the home she shared with her mother and stepfather on Club View Drive, west Los Angeles. Born in 1911 in Kansas City, Missouri, Harlow shot to fame in the early 1930s with films such as *Platinum Blond* and *Red Dust*, but died tragically in June 1937 of uremic poisoning when still only 26 years old. The home Harlow shared with her second husband, MGM executive Paul Bern, at 9820 Easton Drive, Benedict Canyon, Beverly Hills, is also haunted. Bern committed suicide by shooting himself in the head (or was murdered by his deranged ex-common-law wife—accounts differ) in the couple's bedroom of this house. His bloodied ghost was allegedly seen in the house by actress Sharon Tate who was staying there in 1966 with Hollywood hairstylist Jay Sebring. Tate not only claimed she saw the apparition of someone she believed was Bern but also "a human form tied to the stair rail, bleeding from slashes to the throat and quite obviously dying." The latter image has been interpreted by many as a premonition of the brutal slayings of Tate and Sebring at the hands of Charles Manson's followers in August of 1969.

The Oatman Hotel in Oatman, Arizona, is said to be haunted by Hollywood stars Clark Gable and Carol Lombard, who spent the first night of their honeymoon there. Lombard, who died tragically in a plane crash in January 1942, is also said to haunt the penthouse suite of the Hollywood Roosevelt Hotel, on Hollywood Boulevard, where she once stayed with Clark Gable. In fact, the Hollywood Roosevelt is home to a plethora of old Hollywood ghosts.

Originally opened in May 1927 and financed by a group that included movie stars such as Douglas Fairbanks Jr. and Mary Pickford, the hotel was temporary home for a number of movie stars during Hollywood's Golden Age. Perhaps the best-known story from the Hollywood Boulevard involves Marilyn Monroe, who stayed there early in her career for a magazine shoot. A full-length mirror, which now stands in the lobby outside the elevators on the mezzanine level, once hung in suite 1200, when Monroe was in residence there. There are one or two tales saying that guests staring into the mirror have seen the glamorous actress's image reflected in its glass, only to turn around and find no one there. Another movie star whose spirit remains at the Hollywood Boulevard is Montgomery Clift, who lived there for three months in 1952 during the last stages of filming *From Here To Eternity*. Guests and employees have occasionally reported feeling the tragic actor's presence (he died of a heart attack on July 23, 1966, at the age of 45), others have heard bugle playing coming from his old room, Room 928, or seen him roaming around the hallways of the ninth floor.

The many legends and reported sightings of famous people, only a few of which have been touched on in this chapter, show clearly how deep an impression their lives have made on people's minds. Many of us would like to have met or been close to great queens or famous movie stars, and when the death of the icon removes that possibility, for a few of us a posthumous visit by their phantom is the only way to have any connection with them. If someone walking through an English stately home catches a glimpse of a misty vision in what appears to be a long flowing-gown, it is somehow more satisfying to think they have witnessed the ghost of Anne Boleyn rather than an off duty tourist guide or even the spirit of a lesser mortal. As is usually the case in ghost lore, those who have died tragically young or have suffered a particularly violent death are more likely to come back as ghosts; this is especially true when considering the stories of celebrities returning from the grave. Some psychical researchers are of the opinion that because many famous people possessed forceful personalities or single-minded devotion to their objectives their spirits are more likely to linger on after death. However, it is more probable that, in the case of Hollywood celebrities and English royal ghosts, hotels are cashing in on the association with cultural and national icons by exaggerating or even creating legends and tales to bring in the tourist dollar.

Chapter 5

The Headless Horseman and the Death Coach

Despite being one of the most famous of revenants, the headless ghost is decidedly less common in modern ghost lore than it was a few centuries ago. Though even then there were very few actual "sightings" of headless ghosts; accounts of headless beings originating mainly from folklore, myth, and legend. The most prominent types of this macabre phantom are the headless horseman, the solitary ghost carrying his head under his arm, and the headless spectral coachman. The tradition of the headless ghost is found worldwide in many diverse cultures, and exhibits broadly the same characteristics connected with death and death warnings wherever it is found. Popular tradition attributes such hauntings to the wandering spirits of those who have died by beheading, either by execution or accident, though this is rarely supported by the evidence.

Often the headless ghost returns to haunt localities where a murder has been committed or sometimes the site of a suicide or fatal accident. These revenants usually "walk" at midnight and are sometimes dressed in white, which suggests the clothes of the grave. In their indispensable volume on English folklore, *The Lore of the Land* (2005), Jennifer Westwood and Jacqueline Simpson make the astute observation that the stereotypical heedlessness of ghosts represents "a shorthand way of talking about apparitions, like ghosts being dressed in white." In other words, the headlessness is part of how a ghost is, or was in past centuries, expected to appear. Thus, it would make perfect sense for the headless ghost to speak (as does Sir Thomas Boleyn) and a description by a 19th century Norfolk countrywoman of the phantom Black Shuck as being headless but with saucer eyes, is not a contradiction, but merely a traditional way of succinctly indicating that it is a specter.

Perhaps the origin of this type of revenant can be found partly in the ancient practice of beheading corpses, either in an attempt to prevent the dead from returning to plague the living or in connection with regeneration rituals. One of the oldest headless corpses ever recovered comes from Goat's Hole cave, Paviland, on the Gower Peninsula in South Wales. Misnamed the "Red Lady of Paviland," the burial was of a young man who died some 26,000 years ago, during the Palaeolithic period. The man's bones were deeply stained with red ochre and there were also accompanying grave goods, all suggesting fairly elaborate death rituals, of which decapitation may have been a part. At the remarkable Neolithic settlement of Çatalhöyük, in modern southern Turkey, which originated as far back as 7500 BC, there were a number of headless bodies deposited beneath the floors of buildings (a common burial practice at the site). Examination of one particular burial at the site, "Burial 492"—the remains of a headless adult, revealed that the body had been decapitated and the head taken away long after the body had been placed in position in the burial pit. Perhaps the removal of the skull was intended to symbolize the end of the life of the building, and was removed for burial beneath a new building. Further ancient headless bodies have been found in excavations on the island of Vanatu, in the South Pacific, dating back around 3,000 years, and the Nasca culture (AD 1 to AD 750) cemetery site of La Tiza, on the south coast of Peru. In the latter case, the excavator of the site archaeologist Christina A. Conlee from Texas State University, believes that in one of the burials—that of a male of 20–25 years of age—the head was removed either at the time of death or very soon afterward. She states that "The decapitation of the La Tiza individual appears to have been part of a ritual associated with ensuring agricultural fertility and the continuation of life and rebirth of the community."

Supernatural legend and fiction has had a profound effect on the development and characteristics of the headless ghost. In the medieval Arthurian tale of *Sir Gawain and the Green Knight*, the Green Knight challenges Gawain, a knight of King Arthur's Round Table, to behead him with an axe. This Sir Gawain does, but the huge Knight is undaunted, and immediately stands up, retrieves his severed head, and places it under his arm. The knight then laughs and tells Gawain to meet him on the morning of the following New Year's Day for him to take his turn. In a similar legend, known as *The Carl of Carlisle*, Sir Gawain, along with Sir Kay and Bishop Baldwin, is staying with the Carl (Saxon lord) of Carlisle, in Northern England. Their host turns out to be a violent sadistic giant who puts Gawain and his company through a series of bizarre and cruel tests, which again includes a request for Sir Gawain to behead him. This the Knight reluctantly agrees to, but as soon as his head is separated from his body the Carl returns to his normal height and rejoices at being released from the "false witchcraft," which had forced him to behave so murderously, in the past having killed enough guests "to make five cartloads of bones."

Lore of the Ghost

Perhaps the most direct influence on ghostly accounts of "headless revenants" is European legend and folklore. In *The German Legends of the Brothers Grimm* there is a tale of the Wild Hunt called Hans Jagendteufel ("Jack the-Hunting-Devil"), which relates events said to have taken place in the year 1644. At the beginning of the story, we find this statement: "It is believed that if a man commits a crime punishable by decapitation and it remains undiscovered during his lifetime, he will have to wander around after his death with his head under his arm." An extremely succinct description of the archetypal headless ghost. Hans Jagendteufel describes how, one Sunday morning in 1644, a woman from Dresden was out gathering acorns in a nearby forest. While close to a place called Lost Waters, she heard the loud blast of a hunting horn followed by a heavy falling sound. She turned around to see a headless man wearing a long grey coat and sitting on a grey horse. The apparition wore boots and spurs and had a hunting horn hung over his back. Fortunately for her on this occasion the headless rider passed by without doing her any harm.

The *Dullahan* (also *Durahan, Gan Ceann*), a type of unseelie (wicked) fairy who thunders through the darkened lanes of the Irish countryside, especially in remote parts of counties Sligo and Down, is also relevant here. The Dullahan is usually headless, clad in a black flowing cape, and gallops through the night on a black horse, which spews forth sparks and flames from its nostrils. This terrifying specter also uses a human spine as a whip and carries his head, sometimes said to be luminous, either under one arm or in his right hand like a lantern. The head has a wide hideous grin and by holding it aloft the Dullahan can use it to scan the countryside for mortals about to die. When the Dullahan and his horse come to a halt it is a sign that someone will die. All locks and gates are useless against the Dullahan; the only defence against him is gold. One story from Galway, in the west of Ireland, describes a man who met the fearful phantom and outsmarted him by dropping a gold coin on the road, at which the Dullahan vanished. According to Irish antiquary Thomas Crofton Croker (1798–1854) anyone who has the misfortune to glimpse the mounted specter is rewarded by having a basin of blood thrown in their face or being struck blind in one eye by his whip. In some parts of Ireland, such as County Tyrone, the Dullahan drives a coach drawn by a team of six black horses (see below).

Certainly the most influential piece of fiction as regarding American ghost lore, and the Headless Horseman in particular, is Washington Irving's *The Legend of Sleepy Hollow*. This influential short story, contained in his collection *The Sketch Book of Geoffrey Crayon, Gent.*, was first published in 1820, while Irving was living in Birmingham, England. Irving traveled extensively in Europe where he probably picked up some of the elements he used in the story. Indeed, the headless ghost motif was known in German folklore at least as early as 1505 when it was recorded in a sermon written by Geiler von Kaysersberg, who mentions headless spirits being part of the Wild Hunt. There is a story by German poet Gottfried August Bürger called *Der wilde Jäger*, which was translated by Sir Walter Scott as *The Wild Huntsman* (1796), which may have influenced Irving. Despite these northern European influences, the majority of historians agree that it is from Irving's childhood in New York, where he grew up listening to stories told by Dutch immigrants, and his knowledge of the folk tales and characters of the Hudson Valley area, that the most telling influences on *The Legend of Sleepy Hollow* come.

Irving's dark story of the headless Hessian soldier who rides forth every night through the dark lanes of Sleepy Hollow, and the dénouement of the tale involving a supernatural wild chase through the woods, has had a significant affect on the nature of American hauntings. The influence of Irving's tale on popular culture is evident as recently as 1999, with the release of the Tim Burton film *Sleepy Hollow*, starring Johnny Depp and Christina Ricci. In his 1944 article for *The Journal of American Folklore*, "The Ghosts of New York: An Analytical Study," Louis C. Jones noted 15 examples of the headless ghost motif, in New York alone, including four headless horsemen. Another headless ghost tale was reported to the Western Kentucky Folklore Archive in the 1950s by Robert Morris, a Western Kentucky State College student. This tale is set on a hot, dry August day in the distant past when a rancher was sending his entire herd of cattle to the railroad at Cheyenne. Some way into the long journey the cowboys decided to take a much-needed rest. While searching the horizon with his field glasses the trail boss spotted what looked to be a headless rider. After giving the glasses to another cowboy to confirm the strange sight the two rode off in search of the phantom, only to discover no trace of a horse or rider. Returning to camp the cowboys discovered that their herd had vanished leaving no tracks behind them. There is a tradition that on hot summer nights in Wyoming you can still see the headless horseman leading the lost cattle over the Wyoming hills.

In the mid 1960s in the United Kingdom, Ian Rodger collected accounts of no less than five different headless horsemen from a single village (Brill in Buckinghamshire), who roamed the four roads and one field track leading into the village. One of these phantoms was said to be a Roman soldier galloping down toward the village from a nearby Roman marching camp, another a ghostly cavalier who appeared near a 16th-century manor, and yet another, the highwayman Dick Turpin. Further reports of headless horsemen from the United Kingdom include one riding a black steed who patrols Tyndall Avenue on the campus at the University of Bristol, another who trots down the High Street in the village of Pettistree, Suffolk, and another who again rides down the High Street, this time in "England's most haunted village," Pluckley in

Kent. Two more examples of this headless specter come from North Staffordshire. The first gallops along the road from Onecote over Butterton Moor to Warslow, seated on a white horse. It is said that he is either the ghost of a peddler murdered by robbers who cut off his head and placed his body on a horse, or the spirit of a knight killed in battle with the Scots, whose horse brought his headless body home. After meeting this phantom horseman at a crossroads in the 1930s, one countryman is said to have exclaimed, "A man on a horse without a yed on, an awful gory sight!" The other Headless revenant is clad in armor and rides a spectral white horse on the road from Alton to Farley.

Headless ghosts are not confined to horsemen. In a letter to the editor of the English journal *Folklore*, in March 1939, a Mrs. J.M. Biggs recalled that, in 1908, there were stories of a headless ghost in a lane running along the River Stour, close to Tuckton Bridge, at Southbourne in Hampshire. She states that early one evening while walking along the lane she noticed a man sitting on a field gate "leaning towards the river (as I thought) as if on the lookout for someone in a boat." As she drew nearer to the man she noticed that he was headless. Briggs states that she knew nothing of the ghostly tradition associated with the place, and later mentions being told a story about a governess at Wick House in the town who "had a clandestine affair with a handsome groom whom she threw over for a more eligible suitor, whereupon the groom disappeared, his headless body being found in the river many months later."

The headless woman is a relatively common form of phantom found in English ghost lore, and often serves as a death warning. In the 1880s at Alveston, Warwickshire, a ploughboy named Charles Walton is said to have met a phantom black dog on nine successive evenings while making his way home from work. On the final occasion, the dog was accompanied by a headless lady in a silk gown who rushed past him. The following day Walton heard that his sister had died. One case reported by antiquarian and folklorist Sabine Baring-Gould, and carried in the very first issue of *Folklore* in March 1890, describes a phantom at Dalton, North Yorkshire. A tramp was asleep in an old barn in the village when he was awoken at midnight by a light. Sitting up he saw a woman approaching him from the other end of the barn, carrying her head in her hands as if it were a lantern, "with light streaming out of the eyes, nostrils, and mouth." Horrified, the tramp immediately sprang to his feet and broke a hole in the barn wall in his desperation to escape. Baring-Gould adds, "This hole I was shown some years ago. Whether the barn still stands I cannot say." It is not recorded whether the headless apparition served as a death-warning on this occasion.

In the village of Duddon, in Cheshire, northwest England, there is a pub named the Headless Woman, and its signboard shows a woman with her severed head under her arm. In 1866, writer Jacob Larwood mentioned that the pub displayed a notice, which purported to recount the origin of the headless woman sign:

A party of Cromwell's soldiers, engaged in hunting down the Royalists in the Chester district, visited Hockenhall Hall, but found that the family being warned of their coming had buried all the silver and other valuables and then fled for safety, leaving only a faithful old housekeeper in charge of the Hall, thinking it unlikely that the soldiers would do her any harm. The soldiers, being incensed at finding nothing of value, locked up the housekeeper in the top room and proceeded to torture her to tell them where the valuables were hidden. She remained faithful, and was finally murdered by the soldiers cutting off her head. Tradition says that afterwards, on numerous occasions she was seen carrying her head under her arm, walking along the old bridle path between Hockenhall Hall and the spot where it comes out on the Tarporley Road near the public house.

As spookily macabre as this story is, the origin of the pub name has a much more prosaic explanation. Inn signs displaying an image of a headless woman were often used by pubs with names such as the Silent Woman or the Quiet Woman, and derive from a joke aimed at women who talked so much that only the loss of their head could silence them. One such example is the Quiet Woman in the hamlet of Earl Sterndale, Derbyshire, where the inn sign depicts a headless woman, with the words "Soft words turneth away wrath" written where the head should be. The inn sign is reputed to depict a woman known as "Chattering Charteris," the wife of a former pub landlord, who nagged him so incessantly that he sliced off her head. Apparently she was not too popular in Earl Sterndale, as the approving villagers even contributed to the cost of her headstone.

Writing in *The Journal of American Folklore* (January–June, 1941), Grace Partridge Smith describes the headless ghost of a woman who haunted the "hilly, rather wild region on the outskirts of the Shawnee Forest Preserve," in southern Illinois. Apparently this headless specter was often encountered, though she seems never to have appeared in the same way twice, either that or there was more than one headless lady. Stories about the apparition describe her both wearing a black dress and as being red-haired and dressed in a long white robe. According to one tale mentioned by locals, the spectral woman who haunts the area was once the wife of a horse thief who was hung "not so long ago" from a cottonwood or sycamore tree near a flat stretch of road called Drury Bottom. The country people of the area believed that the headless woman came back to haunt her old neighbors, though it seems odd that it is the spirit of the wife and not of the executed man, which comes back as a headless ghost.

A particularly common form of the spectral apparition, especially in Britain and Ireland, is the Phantom or Death Coach. The origins of this particular motif can perhaps be traced back to the *Herlething* (Wild Hunt) of northern, western, and central Europe described in a previous chapter, and the ominous "hell waine," a wagon that carried off the souls of the damned, recorded by Reginald Scot in *The Discoverie of Witchcraft* (1584) as among apparitions common at the time. In later ages, the *Herlething* was transformed in popular lore into the spectral huntsman and his hounds, and this motif itself was gradually superseded by the spectral coach with its headless driver and horses, the driver sometimes being identified as the Devil. This phantom vehicle is also known as the Death Coach, because it often serves as a death omen for someone important (or wicked) in the locality where it is seen, and also because of its black color. The coach, which usually travels rapidly and noiselessly at night along country roads and sometimes across fields, is an ominous thing to witness. Occasionally, especially in Ireland, the Death Coach is only heard rumbling along the lane and not seen.

Writing in *Folklore* in December 1942, Mrs. Cowie notes more than 60 examples of phantom coaches in England, and there are many others that have been discovered by researchers since that date. In the English spectral coach stories, the driver of the coach, if there is one who can be identified, is frequently a local landowner or perhaps a notorious individual of the area. One of the best-known Death Coach stories is that from 17th-century Blickling Hall in Norfolk. This English country house was once owned by Sir Thomas Boleyn, Earl of Wiltshire, and his wife, Elizabeth. Their daughter Ann became the second wife of King Henry VIII in January 1533, only to be arrested on trumped up charges of adultery, incest, and treason; beheaded on May 19, 1536. In *Notes and Queries* (Number 29, May 18, 1850), the Reverend E.S. Taylor describes a story about the ghost of Sir Thomas:

> The spectre of this gentleman is believed by the vulgar to be doomed, annually, on a certain night in the year, to drive, for a period of 1,000 years, a coach drawn by four headless horses, over a circuit of twelve bridges in that vicinity... Sir Thomas carries his head under his arm, and flames issue from his mouth. Few rustics are hardy enough to be found loitering on or near those bridges on that night; and my informant averred, that he was himself on one occasion hailed by this fiendish apparition, and asked to open a gate, but "he warn't sich a fool as to turn his head; and well a' didn't, for Sir Thomas passed him full gallop like:" and he heard a voice which told him that he (Sir Thomas) had no power to hurt such as turned a deaf ear to his requests, but that had he stopped he would have carried him off.

The warning to turn "a deaf ear to his requests" is a common motif in supernatural lore, where it is often recommended not to acknowledge or speak to apparitions, the Devil, or fairies.

Why Sir Thomas, who died a natural death in 1539 at his family mansion of Hever, in Kent, should career around Blickling Hall as a headless specter is hard to explain. Perhaps rumors of his unbridled ambition and alleged refusal to help his daughter and her brother George Boleyn (Viscount Rochford), when both faced execution, endowed him in the minds of the country folk with this ferocious character. Sir Thomas is not the only headless ghost at Blickling. On the anniversary of her execution, Anne Boleyn's ghost, dressed all in white, her bloody head in her lap, is also said to haunt Blickling Hall, riding down the avenue in a phantom coach drawn by four black headless horses.

Fitzford House, near Tavistock in Devon, is home to another female headless ghost. According to local tradition, the Lady Frances Howard (who died in 1671), wife of the owner of Fitzford House Sir Richard Granville, had murdered her first three husbands. Because of these wicked acts she was condemned to ride out every night at midnight in a coach of human bones with skulls at the four corners, driven by a headless coachman, and pulled by four headless horses. A spectral black hound, sometimes said to be Lady Howard herself, with a single eye in the middle of its forehead, also accompanies this terrifying apparition. When the phantom coach arrives at Okehampton Castle it is the strange task of this dog to pluck one blade of grass from the castle mound and bring it back to the gate of Fitzford House. The hound must continue to do this every night until all the grass has been plucked from the mound, which of course will never happen as the grass grows faster than the dog can work. In some versions of this tale, the coach stops to pick up the souls of the dying, which surely indicates that similar to so many spectral coach tales, Lady Howard's phantom coach is the personification of death itself. As Devon folklorist Theo Brown has pointed out, Lady Howard did not in fact own a coach, and as the country folk of Devon in the late 17th century would not have known what such a vehicle looked like, much less encountered one, the phantom coach motif must have been added to her story at a much later date.

In Irish lore the phantom or death coach is usually known as the "Coach-a-Bower" (*Coshta Bower*). Because it is sometimes attached to certain families as an omen of death, the Coach-a-Bower is associated with both the banshee and the Dullahan, the latter sometimes said to be the driver of this phantom vehicle. In the late 19th century, antiquary Thomas J. Westropp collected five stories of the Coach-a-Bower from County Clare, on the west coast of Ireland. The general theme of these stories is that when the Coach-a-Bower is seen or heard all gates should be thrown open, so the phantom will not stop at the house to claim a member of the family, but pass by and so foretell the death of a relative at a distance. On the night of December 11, 1876, a servant of the MacNamaras at Ennistymon House (now The Falls Hotel) was out at Ennistymon in "a beautiful spot in a wooded glen, with a broad stream falling in a series of cascades" (the River Inagh, which runs through the village of Ennistymon, and has some small rapids known as "the Falls"). The man heard the rumbling of wheels along the lane and realized that no "mortal vehicle" would be abroad at such a late hour in that place. He realized it must be the Death Coach, so he quickly ran to open the three gates to Ennistymon House before throwing himself down on his face as the spectral vehicle went clanking past him. It did not stop at the house and its sound gradually disappeared into the night. On the following day Sir Admiral Burton MacNamara died in London.

Lore of the Ghost

In certain parts of France, particularly Brittany, in the northwest of the country, there are tales of a skeleton ghost called "the Ankou" (*Karrigell an Ankou*), who travels about the country at night in a creaking cart or coach drawn by four black horses picking up the souls of the recently departed. According to local belief, the last man to die in a parish in a particular year will become the Ankou for the following year. In stories of the Ankou it is usually the sound of squeaking wheels along the roadway outside one's house that heralds the arrival of this Breton personification of death's servant. Traditionally the Ankou is tall, and wears a wide-brimmed hat and long dark coat, and is accompanied by two skeletons that follow behind his rattling cart tossing the dead into it.

In the United States, as would be expected, phantom coach stories very much echo those of England and Ireland. John Q. Anderson published an interesting spectral coach story from Ayish Bayou, East Texas, in *American Folklore* for October 1963. Although this story has some of the hallmarks of Anglo-Irish lore, it has obviously been influenced by 19th-century romantic fiction. The coach is not black for example, but gold, and there are no horses, headless or otherwise. The events occurred before the Civil War, and the tale was told by an eyewitness, a colored coachman named Ben Smiley. The story involves a local planter's daughter who met a young man at a social gathering. The two fell in love and became engaged. On the night of their engagement, "in the light of the full harvest moon" the young couple decided to take one of the coaches parked outside the girl's house and go for a ride across the country side. But neither the coach nor the young couple were ever to return. Years later, when the couple were forgotten by everyone but their families, the parents of the missing girl were holding another "social" at their home. The coachmen were gathered outside the house talking when one of them happened to glance toward the darkened bayou, only to see "a golden, shapeless glow" noiselessly approach them, within which they could make out the shape of an old-fashioned coach, without horse or driver. As the apparition came closer the terrified group was able to discern the vague shape of a woman inside as the spectral vehicle silently passed by and faded into the autumn night. After that night, every full moon "the golden coach with its spectral passenger silently moved up the drive to the lost girl's home and continued to do so until her parents died." After that, the strange vision was seen no more.

Chapter 6

Visions of the Dying: Crisis Apparitions

A "crisis apparition" is the ghost or apparition of a dead or dying person that is said to appear (usually within 12 hours of death) to a close friend or a relative of the deceased. The apparition can appear in a dream or vision, sometimes interpreted as an actual event, and can occur before or after death has taken place. Though the "crisis" in question may be serious illness or injury, most crisis apparitions occur in cases of sudden death, such as fatal accidents, and last for a very short period, usually a few seconds. Many psychical researchers believe the crisis apparition results from the need of the dying person, often many miles away from the recipient, to communicate their death to their loved ones or simply to say goodbye.

One of the earliest records of a crisis apparition concerns General Joseph Sabine, a professional soldier and governor of Gibraltar, who died at Gibraltar on October 24, 1739, aged 78. The massive, ornate marble tomb of the general was once located in the churchyard of St. Peter's church in the village of Tewin, Hertfordshire, England, but has since been moved inside the church itself. A strange story regarding Sabine's first wife, Hester Whitfield, was recounted in a letter written on November 20, 1759, and printed in the *Gentleman's Magazine* in 1783. According to the letter, the general was once seriously ill after a battle abroad and was lying in his bed one night recuperating, when he saw the curtains at the foot of his bed drawn back and the figure of his wife standing there. After a few moments she vanished. Sabine was understandably affected by this vision, and wrote down the experience in his notebook. Shortly afterward, news arrived that his wife Hester had died in England, at the exact time she had appeared to her husband.

During the late 19th century, an attempt was made by members of the Society for Psychical Research in England to apply modern scientific techniques and standards of investigation to cases that appeared to show the existence of life after death. Indeed, much of the motivation for the research undertaken by senior members of the Society, such as Edmund Gurney, F.W.H. Myers, Frank Podmore, and Eleanor Mildred Sidgwick, was to discover whether there was any sound evidence for the existence of life after death. Consequently, a large number of crisis apparitions were examined by the Society, some of which are detailed in the book *Phantasms of the Living, Cases of Telepathy Printed in the Journal of the Society for Psychical Research During 35 Years*, first published in 1886. One such case was reported to the Society in the form of a letter written by a 42-year-old woman, Miss Lucy Dodson, on September 14th, 1891, regarding an incident that had taken place in her London home several years earlier, on June 5th, 1887:

> ...between eleven and twelve at night, being awake, my name was called three times. I answered twice, thinking it was my uncle, "Come in, Uncle George, I am awake," but the third time I recognised the voice as that of my mother, who had been dead sixteen years. I said, "Mamma!" She then came round a screen near my bedside with two children in her arms, and placed them in my arms and put the bedclothes over them and said, "Lucy, promise me to take care of them, for their mother is Just dead.' I said, 'Yes, mamma." She repeated, "*Promise* me to take care of them." I replied, "Yes, I promise you;" and I added, "Oh, mamma, stay and speak to me, I am so wretched." She replied, "Not yet, my child," then she seemed to go round the screen again, and I remained, feeling the children to be still in my arms, and fell asleep. When I awoke there was nothing. Tuesday morning, 7th June, I received the news of my sister-in-law's death. She had given birth to a child three weeks before, which I did not know till after her death.

Miss Dodson mentioned in her letter that at the time of the incident she was "out of health, and in anxiety about family troubles," and also that she had previously had other, what would now be termed "paranormal," experiences during difficult periods of her life. Such experiences, which included "having felt a hand laid on my head, and sometimes on my hands" would appear to suggest that Miss Dodson was a particularly sensitive individual, and perhaps more likely to witness a "crisis vision" than most. However, she insisted in her communications with the Society that she was awake at the time of the incident, and also that she had never hallucinated before. There is another curious fact, not uncommon in crisis cases, which is that the apparition of her sister in law seemed to exhibit a definite knowledge of her own death, and appeared to be trying to communicate this to Miss Dodson.

One particularly interesting case from the *Proceedings of the Society for Psychical Research* (Volume VII, 1892, p.32) was also recorded by psychical researcher G.N.M. Tyrell in his book *Apparitions* (1953). This story concerns a certain Mrs. Paquet, whose brother was a stoker in a tug working in the Chicago harbor. One morning Mrs. Paquet awoke in a gloomy and depressed mood, which she found impossible to shake off. She went to the pantry for some tea, but when she turned around she saw the image of her brother standing just a few feet away:

> The apparition stood with back toward me, or, rather, partially so, and was in the act of falling forward—away from me—seemingly impelled by two loops or a loop of rope drawing against his legs. The vision lasted but a moment, disappearing over a low railing or bulwark, but was very distinct. I dropped the tea, clasped my hands to my face, and exclaimed, "My God! Ed is drowned."

Shortly after this strange vision Mrs. Paquet received the news that her brother had fallen overboard and drowned, exactly in the manner she had seen it happen, but about six hours earlier.

Visions of the Dying: Crisis Apparitions

In her book *Haunted England* (1940), folklorist Christina Hole relates the story of a crisis apparition case from 1893. On June 22nd of that year, Lady Tryon was entertaining guests at her home in Eaton Square, London, when some of the guests, though not all of them, were amazed to see the figure of her husband Admiral Sir George Tryon, enter the drawing room and proceed to walk silently across it. The Admiral was supposed to be commanding the Mediterranean Squadron off the coast of Syria when his apparition appeared, and Lady Tryon's guests (she does not appear to have seen him herself) were at a loss to explain his presence in London. In fact, at the time of the apparition the Admiral's ship, the *H.M.S. Victoria*, was at the bottom of the Mediterranean, after it was sunk in an accidental collision with another Royal Navy battleship, the *H.M.S. Camperdown*. Half of her crew, including the Admiral, were lost in the sinking.

Crisis apparitions were reported in the hundreds during periods of war, the incidents very often including dead or dying servicemen communicating with loved ones thousands of miles away. One particular apparition was that of English war poet Wilfred Owen, who was serving on the Western Front and was killed while attempting to lead his men across the Sambre-Oise Canal at Ors in northern France. Owen's family received the news of his death a week after it happened, on November 4, 1918, Armistice Day. On the same day Wilfred's brother Harold was an officer aboard the cruiser *HMS Astrae,* anchored in Table Bay near Cape Town, South Africa. The captain of the ship was holding a party to celebrate the end of the War, but Harold was too concerned about the safety of his brother to enjoy himself. Some time later, the cruiser was lying off the coast of the

Cameroons in West Africa; Harold had contracted malaria and had gone to his cabin to write some letters. Suddenly an apparition of Wilfred appeared in his chair, dressed in a khaki uniform. Harold later described the experience in his biography *Journey From Obscurity, Memoirs of the Owen Family. Wilfred Owen, 1893–1918:*

> ...his eyes which had never left mine were alive with the familiar look of trying to make me understand; when I spoke his whole face broke into his sweetest and most endearing dark smile. I felt not fear...I must have turned my eyes away from him; when I looked back my cabin chair was empty...I wondered if I had been dreaming but looking down I saw that I was still standing. Suddenly I felt terribly tired and moving to my bunk I lay down; instantly I went into a deep oblivious sleep. When I woke up I knew with absolute certainty that Wilfred was dead.

Writing in the journal *Western Folklore* for July 1960, Grover C. Allred relates three stories on the subject of the appearance of the ghosts of the dead or dying to friends and relative, told to him in the early 1940s, around the town of Como, northeastern Texas. One of these stories was told by a tenant farmer who had spent his life farming near Winnsboro, Texas:

> Mr. B—and several friends were sitting on the front porch one summer evening. The twilight had already begun to turn dark when they saw a man walking along the public road. He turned into the dooryard and they recognized him to be a neighbor who had gone to Arizona to work. There was

the usual round of conversation and questioning for a while. Then the newcomer said that he had to hurry on to his relative's house about a mile down the road. He never got there, and the next day his relative received notice that he had been killed in Arizona in an automobile accident.

Allred notes in his article the existence of the crisis apparition as a genuine folklore motif "not many years ago in Texas and Missouri." His research also suggested that this motif was then, in the early 1960s, still alive in some of the more remote parts of Missouri, Arkansas, Oklahoma, Texas, and possibly Louisiana.

A more modern account of a typical crisis apparition was reported to Anne Bradford, and published in her *Worcestershire Ghosts and Hauntings* (2001). A woman, who Bradford gives the pseudonym Josie, and her husband lived near the center of the village of Studley, in Warwickshire, and were particularly close to the husband's 98-year-old aunt, who lived in London.

The couple also had a dog that was rather attached to the old lady. One morning Josie was in bed and her husband was in the garden when she heard the dog barking. The husband looked to see what the dog was barking at and saw, to his disbelief, the apparition of his aunt. The old lady was smiling at him and appeared only in black and white "looking as if she had walked out of a black and white television" and was surrounded by a kind of aura. The image of the man's aunt soon faded away, and the couple later learned that she had died soon after this appearance.

The most popular theory for crisis apparitions amongst psychical and paranormal researchers is that the person who is dying or seriously ill acts as the "sender" and telepathically transmits an image of themselves to a loved one—the "receiver." It is believed that the sender is probably unaware that they are sending out a message, though in most cases of crisis apparitions, those involving the death of the sender, this is of course impossible to verify. The obvious difficulty with such a theory is that telepathy has never been proven to exist, and skeptics would argue that there is no hard evidence for the reality of such apparitions outside the minds of the percipients. Believers may insist that the information conveyed by the ghost regarding a tragedy sometimes thousands of miles away, which is unknown to the percipient, is proof of the reality of the apparition. However, it is possible that, in many tales of crisis apparitions, the coincidence between the time of the death of a person and the appearance of their ghost was an element added onto the end of the story at a later date, to give it an air of authenticity.

Some cases of crisis apparitions, as well as some other types of ghosts, may well be explained by visual and auditory hallucinations experienced during the hypnagogic state—the period when the brain is falling asleep after being awake, or the hypnopompic state—when the brain is waking up from sleep. If a person is lying down, or sometimes when sitting, and is in a particularly relaxed state of mind, chances of such hallucinations are significantly increased. It is interesting to note that a large percentage of the crisis apparitions recorded in *Phantasms of the Living* were experienced by people who had just woken up. Of course not all crisis apparitions can be explained as hallucinations, and there remain a few cases where it is difficult to account for the information obtained by the percipient regarding the death of a loved one, though this does not necessarily indicate the existence of telepathy.

Chapter 7

Tales of Doppelgängers and Bilocation

There are various names for the "double," the type of apparition that appears to be the ghostly counterpart of a living person. There are, however, only slight differences between these various sub-types of double. Most appear to be harbingers of bad luck and are even believed to be signs of the imminent demise of the person whose apparition appears. The word *double* itself is used to describe a living person who is reported to be in two different places at the same time; and on a number of occasions the double is actually mistaken for the real person. Similarly, the *doppelgänger*, a German word that translates as "doublewalker" or "doublegoer," signifies an apparition which acts in the same way as another person. This ghostly apparition often haunts its living counterpart, behaving as an "evil twin," and is also known as a "fetch" or "wraith" in British and Irish folklore. The double in general is closely linked with "crisis" or "death bed" apparitions, discussed in Chapter 6. Also related to the double is "bilocation," a term used to describe the ability or phenomenon involved when the individual appears to divide themselves in two, as it were.

One of the earliest reports of a double concerns the apparition of Queen Elizabeth I of England (1533–1603) and was recorded in *The Life of Queen Elizabeth* by Agnes Strickland (1844):

> As her mortal illness drew towards a close, the superstitious fears of her simple ladies were excited almost to mania, even to conjuring up a spectral apparition of the Queen while she was yet alive. Lady Guildford, who was then in waiting on the Queen, leaving her in an almost breathless sleep in her privy chamber, went out to take a little air, and met her Majesty, as she thought, three or four chambers off. Alarmed at the thought of being discovered in the act of leaving the royal patient alone, she hurried forward in some trepidation in order to excuse herself, when the apparition vanished away. She returned terrified to the chamber, but there lay the Queen in the same lethargic slumber in which she left her.

The English Romantic poet Percy Bysshe Shelley (1792–1822) believed he had seen his own double while staying at the Villa Magni, in the Bay of Lerici, northern Italy. In August 1822, Percy's wife Mary Shelley, author of *Frankenstein*, wrote in a letter to her friend Maria Gisborne that one night around two months prior, the poet had burst screaming into her bedroom, apparently still asleep. When he had calmed down, Shelley told his wife that he had had a nightmare in which he met himself while out walking on the terrace, and the double had said to him "How long do you mean to be content?" Shelley was a person with a vivid imagination and had seen many other visions that night, including the image of him strangling Mary. Shelley's vision of his double can be put down to his disillusionment and fraught emotional state at the time—six days before this incident Mary had had a miscarriage, and the couple were going through many other difficulties during this period. Shelley was also reading a drama by the Spanish playwright Calderon, the plot of which revolves around a mysterious stranger who has been haunting the hero his entire life. In the last part of the play, when the stranger is about to fight a duel with the hero, he unmasks and proves to be the hero's own double. The phantom then asks, "Art thou satisfied?" at which the unfortunate man dies of horror.

Carl Sandburg's biography of Abraham Lincoln mentions "a queer dream or illusion," which haunted the president. It was November 6, 1860, and Lincoln had just received news by telegram of his election to the presidency, when he looked into a bureau mirror and saw "himself full length, but with two faces," one paler than the other. Much affected by the apparition, Lincoln got up from the sofa and the illusion vanished, when he sat down again, however, he saw the double again. When he glimpsed his double on another occasion a few days later in the same mirror, Lincoln informed his wife Mary Todd Lincoln of the worrying experience. She told her husband that the vision was a sign that he would be elected to a second term of office, but that the deathly paleness of one of the faces was an omen that Lincoln would not live through the last term, which indeed proved to be the case. One possible explanation for "Lincoln's doppelgänger" is that the mirror into which he looked was an old one, and that his double was an optical illusion. Lincoln was also known to be a superstitious man, and this may have affected his interpretation of the double imagery of the old mirror.

In Welsh folklore, the double or doppelgänger is known under the name of "the Lledrith," which means "illusion." The Lledrith never speaks, and is supposed to vanish if spoken to. This apparition was often regarded as a death omen, though, as the following example illustrates, this was not always the case. This tale, recounted by Marie Trevelyan in her *Folk-lore and Folk-Stories of Wales*, is from near Talgarth, a small market town in southern Powys, Mid Wales:

> A young man...said he once chased his wife for a mile and a half up hill and down dale, until he panted for breath, and was forced to halt, when she vanished. Thinking all this was done for a frolic, he went home, to find his wife quietly seated by the window, knitting. "How did you get back?" he asked. "Get back?" reiterated his wife. "Why, I've never been anywhere!" "Tut, tut! Gwen," said her husband. "You looked as roguish as could be beckoning me from the cherry-tree and out into the road. Then you ran, and I followed a mile and a half, until I could follow no more. I was forced to sit down." "Then you must have followed a Lledrith looking like me, for I have not been outside the doors since you went to the barn after tea.

The "fetch," also known as a "waff" (a version of the "wraith") in the northern counties of England, is a name used in British and Irish folklore to describe another version of the double. In his *Miscellanies* (1696), English antiquarian and writer John Aubrey describes a well-known incident involving such an apparition:

> The beautiful Lady Diana Rich, daughter to the Earl of Holland, as she was walking in her father's

garden at Kensington, to take the fresh air before
dinner, about eleven o'clock, being then very well,
met with her own apparition, habit, and every
thing, as in a looking-glass. About a month after,
she died of the small-pox. And it is said that her
sister, the Lady Isabella Thynne, saw the like of
herself also, before she died. This account I had
from a person of honour.

More commonly in British folklore the fetch occurs in stories about people who foolishly keep watch in the church porch
at midnight on Midsummer Eve or Halloween, in order glimpse
the wraiths of those in the parish doomed to die in the coming
year. In these traditional tales of the fetch, those who keep such
a watch and witness the parade of the dead entering the church
for their funeral service, are horrified to see their own fetch or
double as the first that arrives. The Reverend Robert Kirk, in
his book *The Secret Commonwealth of Elves, Fauns and Fairies*
(1691) calls the double a "Co-Walker," and is of the opinion
that it is one of the fairies. Kirk says that such apparitions are
seen by those with "second sight" (people who would be called
"psychics" nowadays) to eat at funerals and banquets. Kirk also
goes on to say (pp. 69–70):

...they seen to carrie the Beer or Coffin with
the Corps among the midle-earth Men to the Grave.
Some men of that exalted Sight...have told me they
have seen at these Meittings a Doubleman, or the
Shape of some Man in two places; that is, a
superterranean and a subterranean Inhabitant,
perfectly resembling one another in all Points,
whom he notwithstanding could easily one from
another, by some secret Tockens and Operations,

and so go speak to the Man his Neighbour and Familiar, passing by the Apparition or Resemblance of him...They call this Reflex-man a Co-Walker, every way like the Man, as a Twin-brother and Companion, haunting him as his shadow, as is oft seen and known among Men (resembling the Originall), both before and after the Originall is dead; and wes also often seen of old to enter a Hous, by which the People knew that the Person of that Liknes wes to Visite them within a few days. This Copy, Echo, or living Picture, goes at last to his own Herd.

Turning to the closely related subject of bilocation, we find some of the earliest records of this phenomenon in medieval Christian literature. It is the belief of some Catholics that the ability to "bilocate" was bestowed upon a number of Christian saints, mystics, and monks, including St. Ambrose of Milan (338–397), St. Severus of Ravenna (born c. 348), St. Anthony of Padua (1195–1231), and Saint Pio of Pietrelcina (Padre Pio, 1887–1968). One typical example concerns St. Alphonsus Maria de'Ligouri, who on one occasion on September 21, 1774, apparently fell into a trance after saying mass. When he came out of the trance, which lasted a day and a night, St. Alphonsus related that he had visited the bedside of the dying Pope Clement XIV, at least four days travel away. It was later revealed that the Pope had died at 7 a.m., the exact moment when St. Alphonsus came out of his ecstatic state. On a number of other occasions several apparently credible witnesses stated that they had seen St. Alphonsus at two different locations at the same time.

Tales of Doppelgängers and Bilocation

The most famous case of bilocation is undoubtedly that of Emilie Sagée, recorded by politician, author, and spiritualist Robert Dale Owen in his book *Footfalls on the Boundary of Another World* (1859). The story was related to Owen by a Latvian aristocrat named Julie von Güldenstubbe. From 1845–1846 Emilie Sagée, a 32-year-old French-born school teacher, was working at "Pensionat von Neuwelcke," an exclusive girl's school near Wolmar in present-day Latvia. When she was age 13 Julie von Güldenstubbe had been a pupil at this school and told Owen of the strange things that happened around Sagée. Apparently the school teacher had caused much consternation around Pensionat von Neuwelcke by often being seen in two places at the same time. On one occasion, when Sagée was writing on the blackboard in front of 13 students, her exact double appeared next to her and proceeded to mimic her actions, though it did not hold any chalk. At dinner one evening, a similar incident occurred when Sagée's double appeared behind her copying the movements of her eating, although it held no utensils. Sometimes there was a considerable distance between Sagée and her doppelgänger. On one occasion, she was in the school's garden gathering flowers while another teacher sat on a chair in front of the entire body of 42 pupils, who were together in the school hall for their sewing and embroidery lessons. Suddenly, Sagee's double appeared in the teacher's chair while her "real" self could still be clearly seen outside in the garden. The students noticed that while the double sat motionless in the chair, Sagee moved around in a somewhat tired fashion out in the garden. Two girls plucked up the courage to touch the ghost in the chair and apparently felt a slight resistance. One of them then stepped in front of the chair and walked right through a part of the apparition, before it slowly vanished away. The Emilie Sagée case is indeed a fascinating one, though one wishes there were more varied and reliable sources for the events than a single witness whose testimony was recorded 14 years after they allegedly occurred.

Some modern researchersof the paranormal (Hilary Evans, for example) consider that there may be a connection between the double and the so called "astral body," a subtle or "spirit" body, which is said to exist alongside the physical body, as a vehicle of the soul or higher consciousness. Under some circumstances, the theory goes, this astral body can become separated from the physical body. When this separation occurs, during a process known as "astral travel," then this voyaging spirit body may account for sightings of the doppelgänger or double. There has been some recent scientific work that may indicate an interesting psychological aspect to the doppelgänger or double phenomenon.

In September 2006, the journal *Nature* published a paper written by Dr. Shahar Arzy and colleagues from the University Hospital, Geneva, Switzerland, which posited a cause for the eerie feeling people sometimes have that someone is next to them when there is really no one there. Experimenting with a 22-year-old woman with no history of psychiatric problems, and who was, at the time, undergoing pre-surgical evaluation for epilepsy treatment, the doctors stimulated a certain spot in her brain with electricity. The doctors found that, as in certain aspects of the case of Emilie Sagée, the patient described an illusory or shadow person that closely mirrored changes in her own body position and posture. Arzy and his colleagues suggest that disturbance of a site on the brain's left hemisphere evokes the uncanny sensation that there is a double hovering nearby. Though this illusion of a shadow person triggered by the brain cannot explain all cases of the double, obviously not those in which the apparition is claimed to have been seen by others, the results of Dr. Arzy's fascinating research certainly indicates that some cases of the doppelgänger may have their origin in the left temporoparietal junction of the brain.

Chapter 8

The Vanishing Hitchhiker

Though broadly a part of the returning-ghost motif in ghost lore, the Vanishing, or Phantom, Hitchhiker, is best known as a classic urban/contemporary legend. The tale appears to be widespread throughout the world, and though most published examples come from the United States and the United Kingdom, there are also cases from Sweden, Romania, East Africa, and various other countries. Though the story has many variants, the most well-known version generally involves a young vulnerable-looking girl who stands at the edge of a lonely road late at night and hitches a ride from a passing motorist, usually a lone male. The girl usually sits in the back seat and in some cases is completely silent for the whole trip, while in others she asks the driver to take her to a certain address. At some point during the journey the girl mysteriously vanishes while the car is in motion. Later the driver decides to go to the address given to him and inquire about the strange girl, but after giving a description of his passenger he learns that although she did indeed once live at the house, the girl had died in a car crash months or even years before. The fatal accident had often occurred on the very same date and in the exact spot where she was hitching a lift.

The first detailed study of the Vanishing Hitchhiker legend was undertaken by two American anthropologists, Richard K. Beardsley and Rosalie Hankey, and published in the first issue of *California Folklore Quarterly* (now *Western Folklore*) in October 1942, under the title "The Vanishing Hitchhiker." In this detailed article, based on a collection of 79 Vanishing Hitchhiker stories gathered from 60 different locations in the United States, the authors proposed four distinct main types of the Vanishing Hitchhiker legend. Version A of the tale (49 of Beardsley and Hankey's examples fell into this category), is the classic Vanishing Hitchhiker urban legend described previously. These were stories where the hitchhiker is given a ride by a motorist, gives an address, and then disappears. The driver calls at this address only to discover that the passenger has been dead for years. He then realizes he has given a ride to a ghost. The far less common Version B (nine examples) tales are rather different. Here an old woman hitchhiker who is given a ride by a traveler issues a prophecy about a coming catastrophe (in some of Beardsley and Hankey's cases this warning concerned WWII) and then disappears from the vehicle. The driver later discovers that the woman has been dead for some time.

In Version C (11 examples) in Beardsley and Hankey's classification system a young man meets a girl at a place of entertainment, often a dance, and offers to drive her home. On the way the girl complains of feeling cold and the motorist offers his coat or jacket, and she then asks to be dropped off at a cemetery and disappears. The motorist later discovers that the girl he met was, in fact, dead. This fact is confirmed by the man finding her grave in the cemetery where he left her, with the item of clothing he lent her (or some of her own personal possessions) draped over the tombstone, thus establishing the reality of his own strange encounter with the girl. The final type of Vanishing Hitchhiker tale detailed by Beardsley and Hankey, Version D, has only six examples, all from Hawaii. In this version, a driver encounters a mysterious old lady carrying a basket on the highway and gives her a ride. She disappears from his vehicle during the journey and the driver later finds out that he has given a ride to the Hawaiian Goddess Pele.

It was one of the aims of Beardsley and Hankey during their research to discover, if possible, a connection between the Phantom Hitchhiker legend and a real life incident. They were not able to do this, however, though it was their opinion that tales they collected of Version A were most likely to be "the closest to the original story."

In the six and a half decades since the publication of Beardsley and Hankey's work, a number of folklore scholars have turned their attention to the subject of the Vanishing Hitchhiker. Perhaps the most notable amongst these researchers is Jan Harold Brunvand; professor emeritus of English at the University of Utah, whose book, *The Vanishing Hitchhiker: Urban Legends and their Meanings* (1981), has done much to bring the legend to the attention of the general public. Further study of this particular urban legend has shown that there have been many changes and developments to the Vanishing Hitchhiker tale since Beardsley and Hankey's original article, making their classification perhaps a little too simplistic. The typical hitchhiker is still a relatively young girl, but nowadays there are also a few cases in which the hitcher is a young man. More recent research has revealed that the hitcher is not always the ghost of a road accident victim, but can also have suffered a horrific accidental death somewhere else or be the victim of a murder. There are also stories in which the hitchhikers are identified as aliens, angels, saints, Jesus, and evil spirits. In other words the hitcher may take on the role of whatever supernatural entity the particular culture offers.

Research into discovering the age and origin of the Vanishing Hitchhiker has proven problematic, and it seems more likely now that it is a complex mix of related stories rather than a single legend. The main difficulty in discerning how far back the Phantom Hitchhiker legend goes is deciding how you characterize it. If the element of car travel is dispensed with, often to be replaced by horse-drawn transport, then a history of the mysteriously appearing and disappearing fellow traveler on the road can be traced back hundreds of years. For example, English researcher Michael Goss has discovered an early version of the hitchhiker motif in a story in a manuscript written in 1602 and now kept in Linköping library in southern Sweden. The account, told to author Joan Petri Klint by a vicar friend of his, tells how in February 1602 three travelers were journeying back from Västergötland to the town of Vadstena by sleigh when they encountered a young girl standing at the roadside and gave her a ride. When the party stopped at an inn the girl performed some magic, which included turning a jug of beer into blood, and then made a prophecy about wars and plagues. After this she promptly vanished.

In his article "Hitchhiking Ghosts in New York" in *California Folklore Quarterly* for October 1944, Louis C. Jones quotes another ghost story relevant to early versions of the Vanishing Hitchhiker legend. The tale, which was first published in *Golden Mountain: Chinese Tales Told in California*, edited by Paul Radin (1940), involves a young man who, while out walking, meets a young girl in the road weeping. The girl tells the man that she is lost and asks to be taken home, but when they arrive at the house she vanishes. The girl's father informs the distressed man that this has happened before on many occasions. As Jones notes in his article, this is almost a classic Vanishing Hitchhiker tale "except that it derives from an environment where walking is the commonest means of transportation." Jones quotes a number of interesting Phantom Hitchhiker tales from New York in his article, in particular a version of Beardsley and Hankey's Version B hitchhiker. In the New York tales, the old woman hitchhiker is a nun and her prophecies relate to the date when WWII will end, none of which prove correct. In Kingstone, New York, in 1941, the nun was identified as Mother Cabrini, (Saint Frances Xavier Cabrini, 1850–1917) founder of the Sacred Heart Orphanage, West Park, Ulster County, New York. One particular taxi driver who gave her a ride was rumored to have suffered a nervous breakdown soon afterward. The story of Mother Cabrini got so out of hand in the early 1940s that the churches of the area had to officially deny its truth.

One interesting element that Jones notes in his article is that the coat or jacket left by the hitchhiker, or their names on the tombstone, which serve as "proof" of the incident, are supplemented or replaced in some New York examples by another piece of evidence to verify the tale: that of a photograph of the hitchhiker. Rosalie Hankey, in her article "California Ghosts" (*California Folklore Quarterly*, April 1942), published a few months before her classic article on the Vanishing Hitchhiker, also notes this trait in Californian examples of the story. One particular tale was related to a lecturer, the head of the Coptic Fellowship of America, by a fellow spiritualist who claimed the incident occurred when driving from San Diego to Los Angeles:

Near Laguna Beach he turned into the highway. The humming of the motor had put him half to sleep. He saw a woman hitchhiker and stopped. She was a well-dressed, nice-looking woman in her thirties. She said, "Are you going by way of Long Beach?" He said, "Yes." She said, "I'd like to go to a certain address [the narrator could not remember it]. He said he would take her and she got into the back seat. He drove on till he came to Long Beach. Then he turned to say something, and she was gone. He thought this was very strange and went to the address she had given him. A very old man opened the door and he told his story. The man became angry and tried to close the door, but changed his mind and invited him in hurriedly. The old man seemed quite frantic. The younger man described the woman. Then the old man produced a photograph of her. It was his daughter and she had died quite a while before. He said that many people had seen her at the same place.

Jan Harold Brunvand's previously mentioned book, *The Vanishing Hitchhiker: Urban Legends and their Meanings,* contains a number of more recent Vanishing Hitchhiker tales from the United States. One is a purportedly firsthand account, collected in 1969, and involves a man who was driving from Greenville to Winston-Salem in North Carolina. It was dawn and the man was feeling sleepy, and he suddenly saw a young girl in a long dress standing by the road. When the man stopped and asked if she needed any help the girl told him her date had become angry with her "when she stopped his advances" and made her get out of the car and walk. The girl accepted a lift home though she hardly spoke on the journey. When they arrived at the girl's home the driver discovered that the girl had disappeared. He went up to the house and rang the doorbell. An elderly lady answered the door and when the man asked for Mary, she said "Not again," and explained to the bemused man that Mary had been killed in a car crash, and that he was about the fifth person in eight years that had tried to give her a lift home. Another very similar tale included in Brunvand's book was told by a teenager in Toronto, Canada, in 1973. The incident, which apparently involved one of the informant's girlfriend's best friends and her father, occurred when they were driving along a country road. They stopped to pick up a young girl hitchhiker who told them that she lived in a house about five miles down the road, though for the remainder of the journey she sat in silence staring out of the window. As in the previous case, when they arrived at the girl's house the driver turned around to speak to the girl only to find that she had vanished. The informant's girlfriend and her father knocked at the door of the house to tell the people what had happened, and were informed by the inhabitants that they once had a daughter who looked just like the girl they described. Their daughter had disappeared many years ago when she was hitchhiking in the area where they picked her up that day, which would have been her birthday.

Perhaps the best known Vanishing Hitchhiker story from the United Kingdom is that from Blue Bell Hill, a steep stretch of road between Maidstone and Chatham in Kent, in the southeast of England. Research by investigator Sean Tudor has shown that the earliest printed reference for this complicated case is from the *Kent Messenger* for December 8, 1967. A further article in *The Maidstone Gazette* from September 10, 1968, was based on investigations by local paranormal researcher Tom Harber. This article described the apparition of a mysterious girl who was seen on a number of occasions hitching a lift outside the Lower Bell pub. Motorists who gave her a lift into the center of Maidstone described a young girl who chatted happily throughout the journey before vanishing completely from the moving car. However, although Harber had a number of secondhand accounts of the Blue Bell Hill ghost, he was unable to find a single witness to the hitchhiker even after several months of research. Some years later, however, Harber told author and researcher Michael Goss that he had in fact traced and interviewed no less than a dozen firsthand witnesses to the phantom girl, but that he was unfortunately unable to reveal their identities.

One person who claimed that he did actually see the Blue Bell Hill Hitchhiker firsthand was a local bricklayer named Maurice Goodenough.

Early in the morning of July 13, 1974, Goodenough, then 35-years-old, ran into Rochester Police Station claiming that he had just knocked down a young girl with his car on Blue Bell Hill. He informed the police that the girl had appeared suddenly in the middle of the road and he was unable to brake hard enough to avoid running into her. He immediately stopped the car and jumped out to find the young girl lying in the road with cuts to her forehead and knees. Goodenough wrapped the girl in a blanket (or rug in some versions), carried her to the roadside, and drove off to get help. When he returned to the scene of the accident with the police all they found was the blanket lying on the ground; the girl had disappeared. There were no traces of blood either on the car or on the road, and despite an extensive police search of the area using tracker dogs the young girl was never found. Goodenough described the girl as about 10 years of age, with shoulder length brown hair and wearing a lacy white blouse, white ankle socks, and a skirt. Despite the difference in age between this girl and the hitcher described in

The Vanishing Hitchhiker

The Maidstone Gazette, local tradition considers the two ghosts of Blue Bell Hill as the same.

The explanation put forward for the appearance of this tragic phantom is a crash that occurred on Friday, November 19, 1965, when three of four women traveling in a car were killed when it crashed on Blue Bell Hill. One of the fatally injured women was due to be married next day, though it is believed locally that the hitchhiking ghost actually represents the bridesmaid rather than the bride. According to local newspapers, in November 1992 there were further incidents reported by motorists who believed they had run over a young woman on Blue Bell Hill, only to find no trace of the supposed victim when they looked on the road. As in the previous sightings, searches of the surrounding area by the police proved fruitless, a common outcome in such folkloric tales.

As mentioned earlier in this chapter, the Hawaiian version of the Vanishing Hitchhiker legend involves the goddess Pele. Pele, the Hawaiian goddess of fire, lightning, dance, and volcanoes, has been reported as attending social events such as dances, as does Beardsley and Hankey's Version C hitchhiker. Pele is also said to appear at the roadside as a beautiful young woman or an old woman with white hair, sometimes accompanied by a white dog. It is said that those who give her a ride in their car are blessed, while those who ignore her are cursed. The Bantu culture of the East African Coast, an area significantly influenced by Arab Muslim culture, have stories of malicious supernatural beings known as "jini" (in English "genies"). A jini can take on the form of a beautiful girl who is picked up by a truck driver who at some stage in the journey turns to look at the girl. When he does, however, he finds to his horror that she has goat's legs, whereupon she laughs and disappears. On some occasions, the truck driver is so shocked by the discovery of a jini in his cab that he skids off the road and crashes.

As can be gathered from the majority of examples of Vanishing Hitchhikers tales in this chapter, the stereotypical hitcher could be described as a young innocent girl on the brink of adulthood. This point is, in itself, significant. Gillian Bennett, in her article "The Vanishing Hitchhiker at Fifty-Five" (*Western Folklore*, winter, 1998), proposes a "rites of passage" model to help explain the function of at least one variant of the Hitchhiker stories. She suggests:

> ...the hitchhikers died while separated from one social sphere and before being incorporated into another. We could then argue that they are caught in the transition zone in some sort of endless loop, trying either to progress forwards or to retreat backwards.

Although the Vanishing Hitchhiker is believed by folklorists to be nothing more than an urban legend, some researchers, Michael Goss, for example, believe that there may be something more to the tale than mere fiction. Nevertheless, as Jan Harold Brunvand notes in *The Vanishing Hitchhiker: Urban Legends and their Meanings*, the majority of people are not aware of the large amount of variants on the Hitchhiker story. And, as all folklorists know, and as Brunvand states "multiple, varying texts in oral tradition are good evidence against credibility." With this in mind perhaps the Vanishing Hitchhiker legend is best understood in the context of ghost lore as a whole, where it fits in well with the tradition of the ghost who returns briefly to the land of the living in order to settle unfinished business, to continue an activity they were known to pursue during their lifetime, or, most relevantly, in terms of Vanishing Hitchhiker stories, to escape from their in-between, liminal state and find rest. Whatever its true origin, the fact that the Vanishing Hitchhiker is still discussed and reported today indicates the motif still has meaning and relevance in the folklore and urban legend of modern 21st-century society.

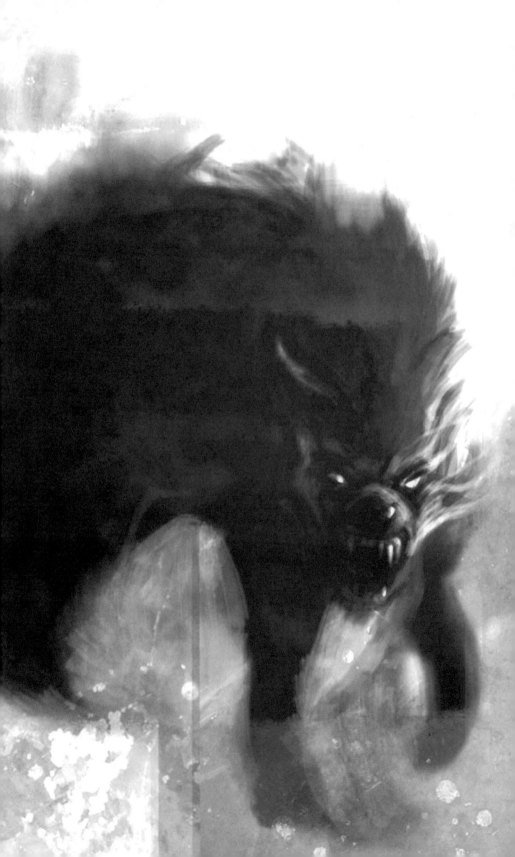

Chapter 9

Black Dogs

A phantom black dog is a supernatural creature found primarily, though not exclusively (there are examples from Latin America and the United States), in British folklore. Black dogs should not be confused with the ghosts of dead pets; they are an entirely different phenomenon. The black dog is generally reported at night, and is usually said to be larger than a normal dog, often possessing shaggy fur and large glowing eyes. Most counties of Britain have their own variant of the black dog. There is the "Black Shuck" of East Anglia; "Trash" or "Skriker" in Lancashire; the "Padfoot," "Bogey Beast," and "Barghest" of Yorkshire; the "Gurt Dog" of Somerset; the "Yeth (Heath)" or "Wisht Hounds" of Devon; and the "Mauthe Doog" of the Isle of Man. Some of these black dogs, Shuck for example, can assume other forms than that of a black dog, and are thus more akin to shape-shifting demons than more traditional black dogs.

The black dog can perform a variety of functions, from acting as a portent of death to representing the ghosts of a deceased person. A gallows site in Tring, Hertfordshire, was said to be haunted by a huge black dog, believed locally to be the spirit of an executed criminal called Thomas Colley. This frightening creature was apparently seen by the village schoolmaster, who described it as being as big as a Newfoundland, with long ears and flaming eyes. Colley, a chimney sweep, had been arrested for his part in the killing of an old woman who had been drowned for witchcraft at Tring in April 1751. He was later hanged and gibbeted near the place of the crime. Black dogs could also be guardians of treasure, such as at Dobb Park Lodge, in Lancashire in north-west England. However, it was not until the late 19th century that the black dog began to be interpreted mainly as a ghost. Previously, it was the diabolic characteristics of these spectral creatures that were emphasized. Indeed, in several accounts of English witch trials from the 16th to 18th centuries the Devil is described as appearing in the form of a black dog. One notable characteristic of the black dog is its association with specific locations, for example ancient trackways, as the abundance of roads called "Black Dog Lane" testify. These phantom creatures are also associated with churchyards, streams, pools, wells, bridges, parish boundaries, and ancient barrows (burial mounds).

Perhaps the best known of Britain's ghostly black dogs is Black Shuck of the eastern counties of Norfolk, Suffolk, and Essex. Also known as "Old Shuck" this creature's name perhaps originates from the Old English *scucca*, a demon. Shuck can appear as a black shaggy dog the size of a horse with glowing red eyes like saucers, though he can also be headless, or, on occasion, invisible. Black Shuck's star appearance came between 9 and 10 on the morning of August 4, 1577, when he is said to have entered St. Mary's

Church, Bungay, in Suffolk, during a violent storm. Shuck was illuminated by flashes of fire as he ran around the church causing mayhem among the worshippers, two of whom he killed instantly and another who he left severely injured. Shortly after this appearance Black Shuck entered Holy Trinity Church, Blythburgh, seven miles away. The fearful creature struck three people dead, burned the hand of another, and left long black scratch or scorch marks on the north church door as it departed. These marks can still be seen today.

These bizarre incidents were first reported in a tract published in 1577 by Abraham Fleming entitled "A straunge and terrible Wunder wrought very late in the Parish Church of Bongay..." The fame of Bungay and Black Shuck began with this pamphlet, which described the "appeerance of an horrible shaped thing" in the church during "a great tempest of violent raine, lightning, and thunder, the like wherof hath been seldome seene." However, the Churchwarden's Books for 1577 make no mention of an appearance of any supernatural creature, merely noting in the margin (as quoted by Jennifer Westwood and Jacqueline Simpson in *The Lore of the Land* (2005) "a great terrible and ferfull tempest at the tyme of procession vpon the Sondaye, such darknes, Rayne, hayle, thunder and lightnying as was never seen the lyke."

Similarly, an account of the great storm in the area published in Ralph Holinshed's *Chronicles of England, Scotland and Ireland* (1577) makes no reference to a black dog. What seems to have happened is that Abraham Fleming, the author of the pamphlet, being a Puritan preacher, was using the incident of the black dog to graphically illustrate a divine punishment for the sins of the congregation. In an age when particularly violent storms were interpreted by some as the Devil's divine punishment for sin, the influence of this pamphlet was considerable.

The story of Black Shuck's appearance at Bungay and Blythburgh is not unique in this era. A Pamphlet written by Luke Hutton and published in 1612, was entitled *The discouery of a London monster called, the black dog of Newgate*. This work related the horrific tale of starving prisoners at Newgate Gaol in London, who were so desperate that they killed other prisoners for food. One of the prisoners they murdered was a sorcerer, and after his death a huge black dog appeared and haunted the area of Newgate Prison. Another pamphlet, *The Wonders of this Windie Winter*, published in 1613, tells how one Sunday during a tempest at Great Chart in Kent, a creature resembling a bull rampaged through the church leaving dead and injured in its wake before it vanished, demolishing part of the church wall as it went. Although some researchers have theorized that such appearances of strange creatures during storms may have been caused by the little-understood phenomenon known as ball lightning, it is more likely, as Jennifer Westwood notes in *Albion: A Guide to Legendary Britain* (1986), that "we [are] dealing with a good tale going the rounds," rather than any real events.

In her article in *Folklore* for June 1938, Ethel H. Rudkin recounts a number of fascinating tales involving black dogs from her native county of Lincolnshire, in the east of England. One of the many interesting conclusions to be drawn from the stories of black dogs in Rudkin's article is that compared to Black Shuck and other examples of this spectral beast, the Lincolnshire variety is relatively harmless. Some examples from her article will demonstrate this and many other pertinent characteristics of Lincolnshire black dogs. At the end of the 19th century a young man who regularly cycled home from Leverton to Wrangle (in the Boston area of the county) would often see a black dog that appeared near a long, deep pond surrounded by trees and disappeared down a lane. Another black dog was frequently reported at Belle Hole, a farm a mile west of Kirton, also in the Boston area, where it was is said to live in a hole in the bank of a stream. This very large black dog was usually seen making its way along an isolated stretch of road up to Kirton, and would often trot alongside people as they walked.

Ethel H. Rudkin describes another appearance of this particular Boston-area beast, where it is referred to as a "boggart" (a kind of fairy or household spirit):

> Some thirty years ago, the monthly nurse had been required at Belle Hole. Her time was up and she was returning to Kirton when she had put the other children to bed. As she was giving them their supper, they were talking of the Boggart—"Aren't yer scared o' meetin' 'im, miss ?" they asked, and " wot'll yer do if yer does meet im ?" and the nurse replied, "I shall put 'im i' my pocket." Later on she was returning to Kirton in the dark, when the Dog appeared and ran round her saying " Put me in yer pocket, put me in yer pocket." This is the only record of the Dog speaking, and the explanation had probably to do with the railway and the direction of the wind, for if the wind were blowing from the north or north-west, the wheels on the line possibly accounted for the "put-me-in-yerpocket, put-me-in-yer-pocket."

As with many other supernatural creatures, the British black dog is frequently associated with boundary features and liminal places, and Rudkin's Lincolnshire examples are no exception. At South Kelsey the beast walks along a road and disappears into a fence. At Manton he is met with on an old lane near the bridge that crosses the stream. At Willingham he is reported along Brick Pit Lane near the bridge that crosses the river Till. The latter apparition was once said by locals to be connected with a woman who drowned herself at this spot.

One example of the shape-shifting variety of British black dogs is the Lancashire (and elsewhere in the north of England) creature known as "Skriker," "Trash," or the "Gytrash." This black dog, in keeping with those of the rest of the country, was said to haunt lonely roads, though this is where the parallels with the more solid black dogs, such as the Lincolnshire examples, end. This creature, more akin to a malevolent fairy than a ghost dog, could assume the shape of a large dog, a horse, or a mule, and would lead travelers astray, much like the ghostly lights discussed elsewhere in this book. The term "Skriker" means *Shrieker*, as the dog was said to utter a fearsome ear-piercing scream, which could be heard even when the creature was invisible. The name *Trash* is said to originate from the padding sound made by the beast's huge feet as it splashed through puddles. Charlotte Brontë refers to a "spirit called a Gytrash" in her 1847 novel *Jane Eyre*.

A similar north of England shape-shifting black dog is the "Barghest." This legendary monster is said to be able to assume a variety of forms, but usually appears as a large, shaggy black dog with huge teeth and claws, fiery eyes, and horns. As with Skriker, the Barghest is more akin to a malicious spirit or goblin than a traditional black dog. Troller's Gill, a limestone gorge in the Yorkshire Dales, is said to be haunted by this monstrous black dog. It was a local belief that anyone who saw the Barghest would die soon afterwards while those who only caught a brief glimpse of the creature may live on for a few months.

Another terrifying canine apparition was the Welsh "Gwyllgi" ("wild" or "twilight" dog) aptly known as "The Dog of Darkness." In his classic work on Welsh traditions, *Folklore of West and Mid Wales* (1911), Jonathan Ceredig Davies describes the Gwyllgi as "a frightful apparition of a mastiff with baleful breath and blazing red eyes." He notes one particular appearance of this creature at Pant y Madog, near the town of Laugharne, Carmarthen:

A woman named Rebecca Adams, passing this spot late one night, fell down in a swoon, when she saw the spectral dog coming towards her. When within a few yards of her it stopped, squatted on its hounchers, "and set up such a scream, so loud, so horrible, and so strong, that she thought the earth moved under her." I was informed at Llangynog five years ago, that Spectral Dogs still haunt that part of Carmarthenshire; and more than one of my informants had seen such apparitions themselves.

The United States also has its fair share of ghostly black dogs. U.S. Route 97, a north-south highway in the western United States, is supposed to be haunted by two black dogs on the stretch of road between Madras and Sunriver, Oregon. An apparition of a black dog with glowing red eyes is said to haunt Sweet Hollow Road, Huntington, Long Island, New York, and is supposed to be a harbinger of death for anyone who witnesses it. This large dog walks on its hind legs and is sometimes known as The Black Dog of Misery, perhaps due to a link with the nearby Mount Misery. Another black dog that acted as a death portent is described by Grace Partridge Smith in her article "Folklore from "Egypt" published in *The Journal of American Folklore*, (January–June, 1941). The informant for this case was a Dorothy Pemberton of the city of Eldorado, Saline County, Illinois. Pemberton reported that a certain family had a tradition that a black dog would come and scratch at their door when anyone was about to die. On one occasion, the family heard scratching and whining coming from the kitchen door and opened the window to take a look. Outside the back door they saw an enormous black dog and sure enough, a short time later, their grandmother died.

A rather unusual black dog haunts the West Peak of Hanging Hills, a range of mountainous ridges overlooking the city of Meriden, Connecticut. Rather than being a large ferocious beast, the black dog of Hanging Hills is a small, silent black dog, which makes no sound even when it appears to bark or howl, and leaves no footprints in snow or soil. Despite its innocent appearance, this dog is again said to act as a death omen, as local tradition asserts that to see the supernatural dog once is good luck, twice results in misfortune, but a third time signifies death. The best known report of the black dog of Hanging Hills was published by New York geologist W.H.C. Pynchon in the *Connecticut Quarterly,* (April–June, 1898). In this account, Pynchon states that he and fellow geologist Herbert Marshall of the U.S. Geological Survey were carrying out research in the Hanging Hills in February of 1891 when they encountered the dog. Both had seen the dog before, Pynchon once and Marshall twice, and as they climbed Marshall slipped on the ice on top of one of the cliffs and plunged to his death. He had seen the dog for a third time. Six years later, Pynchon returned to the Hanging Hills, apparently saying he intended to climb the same peak where Marshall had met his death. He never returned. According to local lore, after an extensive search of the area, Pynchon's body was eventually found in the same ravine where Marshall had fallen. Obviously, Pynchon had seen the black dog a third time and his death was assured. Unfortunately for this neat little piece of folklore-becoming-reality, W.H.C. Pynchon in fact died in Oyster Bay, Long Island, in 1910. Still, reports of the Hanging Hills black dog continue to circulate and the deaths of climbers in the area are often attributed to seeing the fateful dog for a third time.

Latin American folklore also has its phantom black dogs. The "Perro Negro" (Spanish for "black dog") of Latin America, like its British counterpart, is known by a wide variety of names in different parts of the region. Examples include the aforementioned Perro Negro of Mexico, Huay Chivo (Mexico), Cadejo (Central America), Familiar (Argentina), and Lobison (Argentina). In Latin America, black dogs with fiery eyes are usually demonic in nature, regarded as either an incarnation of the Devil or a shape-shifting sorcerer.

Black Dogs

One of the most frequently cited parallels for phantom black dogs are the pack of spectral hounds that accompany the Wild Hunt (see Chapter 1). However, the black dogs discussed in this chapter are almost always solitary, unlike those of the Wild Hunt. Undoubtedly a number of the reported sightings of ghostly black dogs can be explained as flesh and blood animals straying at night, but not all fit this description. The black dog motif certainly fits in well with other supernatural creatures in terms of the places where it is encountered, that is, liminal spots such as roads, hedges, fences, streams, and bridges. It was at such places that the veil between this world and the next was believed to be at its thinnest, and consequently where one would expect to encounter otherworldly creatures such as the phantom black dog. In its role as a portent of death, the black dog also has parallels with other supernatural creatures described in this book, such as the "fetch" or "double," and the headless horseman. The dog's association with death in European mythology should also be borne in mind. Examples include the Cŵn Annwn ("hounds of Annwn")—the spectral hounds of Annwn, the otherworld of Welsh myth; Garm, The Hound of Hel, a watchdog chained to the gates of Under-Earth, the Norse realm of the dead; and Cerberus, the three-headed hound of Hades in Greek myth. Perhaps the dog's role in myth as guardian of the Underworld has left a faint trace in more modern folklore, where the creature patrols certain roads and lanes acting as a kind of guardian spirit. Black dog lore also has parallels with the fairy dogs of British and Irish folklore. The Cu Sith, the enormous fairy dog of Scotland, was reportedly the size of a cow or a large calf, though as befits a fairy hound, it was dark green in color with shaggy fur. The black dog is a powerful archetype and its true origins and meaning are difficult to discern, though its appearance in ghost lore is undoubtedly a result of a complex mixture of folklore, myth, outright fiction, and perhaps even genuine sightings of unknown animals.

Chapter 10

Haunted Houses

The motif of the haunted house is a deep rooted one, perhaps having its origin in the ancient belief that each place, including dwellings, had its own "genius loci," which in Roman mythology meant the protective deity/spirit of a location, but which could also be the place's distinctive spirit. In modern times the haunted house has become a universal phenomenon—almost every town or village in every corner of the world has a building with a reputation for unexplained, often frightening happenings. In past centuries, the house, whether mansion or cottage, was the place where people died. Consequently, the fact that the ghosts of the deceased were said to return to these places, or, in the opinion of some psychic researchers the residual psychic energy or impressions of these previous occupants, is not unusual.

The haunted house need not be the former home of the deceased, it may also be a particularly favorite place or even the house of someone who has caused their death, and is thus haunted by his or her victim's vengeful ghost. The hauntings consist of "supernatural" occurrences including apparitions of the dead person, the unexplained movement of household furniture or other objects (usually associated with poltergeist cases), inexplicable sounds, smells, and uncanny feelings. Such phenomena can be reported as occurring in the same house for days, years, or even centuries. The haunting may be stopped by various methods, including exorcism, prayers, the proper burial of the deceased whose ghost appears, remodeling of the structure, or even the total destruction of the house. In a few cases, however, none of these methods appear to have been successful.

The haunted house has an extremely long history; the motif stretches at least as far back as the Roman period, when authors such as Plautus, Pliny the Younger, and Lucian recorded accounts of buildings plagued by ghosts. Roman senator and author of a famous collection of letters, Pliny the Younger (c.62–c.113 AD), recorded a "true story" of a haunted house in Athens, which was inhabited by a "spectre who came out at night rattling his chains" and who had scared away all the tenants. A philosopher stayed the night at the house in order to get to the bottom of the mystery, and when the ghost appeared to him it beckoned him to follow it into the garden where it promptly vanished. The next day, the philosopher had the local magistrate dig at the spot where the ghost had vanished and a skeleton in chains was discovered. The skeleton was reburied and the haunting ceased. A similar story was told by Greek writer Lucian (born around 120 AD) in his *Philopseudes*, which concerned a house in Corinth haunted by a phantom with the ability to turn itself into a dog, bull, or lion. As in Pliny's tale, this spectre also terrified anyone who attempted to live in the house, that is until a Pythagorean philosopher-mystic visited the place, and, with the aid of his collection of esoteric books, was able to withstand all attempts by the ghost to frighten him away. Finally, using an ancient Egyptian curse the philosopher sent the phantom down into the earth. On the following day, at the spot where the ghost disappeared the night before, a rotting corpse was discovered six feet down. The body was taken out and reburied, and the hauntings duly stopped. As R.C. Finuncane points out in his excellent book on the cultural history of ghosts, *Appearances of the Dead* (1982), these Roman-era cases of haunted houses perform the function of illustrating the superiority of one kind of supernatural philosophy over another, the philosopher with his books triumphing over the dead, and thus death itself.

This idea of one philosophy or faith conquering another is central to the understanding not only of haunted houses, but ghosts in general, especially during the early medieval period. The motif reappears again, this time in an early Christian context in the story of a haunted house visited by Bishop (later saint) Germanus, Bishop of Auxerre, who died in 448. The Bishop's life was recorded by Constantius of Lyon in a work entitled *de Vita Germani* ("on the Life of Germanus"), which was completed some time before 494. In *de Vita Germani* Constantius describes an occasion when the bishop and his party were traveling one night and were forced by the onset of darkness to stay at a dilapidated old house said by the locals to be haunted. After the group had settled in, one of the Bishop's clerics was reading aloud when:

> Suddenly there appeared before the reader's eyes a dreadful spectre, which rose up little by little as he gazed on it, while the walls were pelted with a shower of stones. The terrified reader implored the protection of the bishop, who started up and fixed his eyes upon the fearful apparition. Then, invoking the name of Christ, he ordered it to declare who he was and what he was doing there. At once it lost its

terrifying demeanour and, speaking low as a humble suppliant, said that he and a companion after committing many crimes were lying unburied, and that was why they disturbed the living, because they could not rest quietly themselves.

The ghost led the Bishop to the location of the buried bones and, the following day, the Bishop ordered his men to dig at the spot:

...the bodies were found, thrown down anyhow, the bones still fastened together with iron fetters. A grave was dug in accordance with the Church's law, the limbs were freed from the chains and wrapped in winding sheets, earth was thrown upon them and smoothed down, and the prayers for the dead were recited.

As in the previously quoted cases, after all these rites were performed the haunting stopped.

Moving onto modern era accounts of haunted houses we can see that the phantoms encountered have changed only in the detail. One of the best known haunted addresses in the United Kingdom is No. 50 Berkley Square, in the West End of London, in the City of Westminster. The house was completed in 1740, but it is with the occupancy of an eccentric recluse named Mr. Myers in the 1850s that the sinister reputation of the house seems to have arisen. Mr. Myers had been engaged to be married but was jilted by his bride to be at the last moment, and it was this, according to J.A. Brooks writing in *Ghosts of London*, which drove him mad. He became a recluse, living only in one room of the property, wandering around the upper floors with a candle at night, and allowing the house to fall into decay around him. Such eccentric behavior led to a great deal of speculation among the neighbors and, subsequently, various strange tales arose about 50 Berkeley Square.

According to an article in the magazine *Mayfair* in 1879, the ominous looking property was then known as "the haunted house in Berkeley Square," and during this period its sinister reputation elevated it to a tourist attraction. Through a number of its issues *Mayfair* related various tales of unexplained deaths, black magic, and secret locked rooms connected with the property, one of which concerned a maidservant who was given one of the top-floor rooms to stay in. Shortly after the household had retired to bed one night terrible screams were heard coming from the servant's room on the upper floor, where the girl was found standing motionless in the middle of the floor "with hideously glaring eyes." Apparently the maidservant never regained her sanity nor was able to relate what she had seen that terrified her into madness. A series of correspondences in the journal *Notes and Queries* in the early 1870s on the subject of the house on Berkeley Square added more second- and thirdhand tragedies to the ghost lore of the house. However, there were also letters from various maids who had worked there in the 1850s, during the time of Mr. Myers, all of whom refuted claims of ghostly occurrences at the house. Further stories regarding 50 Berkeley Square emerged through the years, including the familiar haunted house motif that the property was being used by a gang of forgers who started the rumors of the hauntings to conceal their nefarious activities. Another more supernatural tale, told by Elliott O'Donnell in his book *Phantoms of the Night* (1956), concerned two sailors who broke into the house looking for somewhere to stay after a night on the town. During the night the sailor's were awoken by the sound of heavy footsteps and other strange noises and were terrified when the door of their room burst open and a horrible shapeless form confronted them. One of the sailors managed to escape from the terror, but the other was pushed (or jumped) out of a window to die a horrible death impaled on the railings below.

Since 1938, 50 Berkeley Square has been the home of antique booksellers, the Maggs Brothers, and, predictably enough, there have been no encounters with ghosts reported during their tenancy.

Another famous property that seems to be haunted more by rumor than ghosts is the "Winchester Mystery House," a Victorian gothic structure located in San Jose, California. The huge sprawling mansion was built during a 38-year period, beginning in 1884, by Sarah Winchester, the widow of gun magnate William Wirt Winchester (1837–1881) second president of the Winchester Repeating Arms Company. The couple originally settled in New Haven, Connecticut, but in 1866 their baby daughter died when only a few weeks old, followed in March 1881, by the death of William himself of tuberculosis while still only in his 40s. Sarah was distraught after these tragedies and sought the advice of spiritualists. According to tradition, one medium told her that the Winchester family was under a curse from the spirits of the people who had been killed by the Winchester rifle. Sarah was instructed to sell the property in New Haven and head toward the setting sun where she would start a new life by building a home for herself and the spirits of the victims of Winchester rifles. The medium is also alleged to have told Sarah that if she ever stopped building the house she would die.

Though the 1906 San Francisco earthquake damaged the house significantly, when Sarah Winchester died in 1922 the labyrinthine structure still contained around 160 rooms. This huge, eccentric structure with its bizarre history is home to a number of phantoms. Most of these follow the pattern of the stock haunted house tales of mysterious footsteps, banging doors, cold spots, and strange voices. Various psychics have also visited the Mystery House, now a tourist attraction, and most have felt the presence of disturbed spirits and one or two even confirmed that the Winchester Mansion is indeed cursed. Apart from such anecdotal evidence, there are no documents relating to the ghostly stories surrounding the mansion, and its reputation as a haunted house seems to rest entirely on its strange appearance and the curious history of Sarah Winchester.

Another well-known haunted property in the United States is 1340 Pennsylvania Street, Denver, Colorado, the former home of Titanic survivor Molly Brown. The three-story house, built in 1889, is now a museum, and is said to be visited by the ghosts of both Molly and her husband James Joseph "J.J." Brown. Members of the staff have also reported the smell of pipe and cigar smoke, cold spots throughout the property, and the movement of the window blinds in a room that belonged to the couple's daughter, Catherine Ellen. Rosalie Hankey's article on California Ghosts in the *California Folklore Quarterly* (Vol. 1, No. 2. April, 1942), includes a short account of an interesting and somewhat bizarre haunting at an abandoned house between Santa Cruz and Monterey. While out driving, an acquaintance of the narrator and a friend stopped one day to look at the old house:

It was surrounded by a wall. They found a way through the wall and saw that the house consisted of a large central porch surrounded by small connecting rooms giving on the central porch. The woman said that she felt uneasy and did not want to go through the house. Her friend, saying, "Nonsense! Don't be foolish," went into the house alone. The woman, remaining in the central porch, saw her friend passing from room to room, and, deciding that she was being silly, started to follow. As she entered she saw a woman's head floating in midair. She screamed and ran out. Her friend came out and asked, "What's the matter?" But the woman was afraid to tell what she had seen.

Later the woman discovered that the house had been abandoned because of a murder committed by the wife of the owner.

There is very little to add to the story of Britain's most infamous haunted house, Borley Rectory, a Victorian structure which was located in the village of Borley, Essex, in the southeast of England.

The ghostly phenomena reported from the house are a fine selection from the canon of British ghost lore, including a ghostly nun, a phantom coach and black horses, whispering voices, a mysteriously creaking staircase, ringing bells, an unexplained light, "spirit writing" on the walls, and various poltergeist activitiy including showers of stones raining down on the house. The validity of the hauntings at Borley are impossible now to separate from their connection with psychic investigator Harry Price, who took up residence there with a team of mostly student researchers for a year from May 1937. However, the results of Price's investigations at Borley were inconclusive, though he published an account of some of the alleged strange activity at the property in his book *The Most Haunted House in England: Ten Years' Investigation of Borley Rectory* (1940). In 1939, the occupier of the rectory, Captain William Gregson, accidentally tipped over an oil lamp near a bookstand and the old house was gutted by fire. The ruined property was finally demolished in 1944. Price died in 1948, and since then there have been various publications supporting or refuting his theories and findings. What is clear is that if it were not for the notoriety gained for Borley by the publicity-conscious Price, then the relatively anonymous apparitions attested at the property would probably be forgotten today.

A particularly relevant and informative haunted house story is included in David Taylor's article "Spaces of Transition: New Light on the Haunted House," originally published in the journal *At the Edge* (No.10 1998). The story came from a family living in a suburb of Birmingham, in the United Kingdom where, at night, the mother and daughter of the family would hear footsteps walk across the patio behind the house, enter the building (without the sound of a door opening), climb the stairs, and finally stop outside the teenage daughter's bedroom. On investigation nothing was ever discovered to account for the strange sounds. The family enquired locally about the house, and were told that people never lived in the property for very long. When David Taylor visited the family they told him that they believed a past resident who had died in the house was responsible for the haunting. The family also revealed that previous occupants of the house had reported the same unexplained footsteps, hence the reason why no one had ever stayed there long. However, Taylor's research at the local record office showed that, in fact, a normal amount of families had lived in the property for reasonably long periods, and there was no evidence that anyone had ever died in the house. As Taylor notes, this case illustrates an important point about claims of "haunted" properties. When apparently unexplained phenomena occured, the family believed, reinforced by rumors passed on to them by neighbors, that the only possible explanation was that it was the work of the restless ghost of a former resident who died in the house. We can see here that very little has changed in the make-up of the haunted house story from Pliny the Younger's tale 2,000 years earlier. When the idea that a house is or might be haunted becomes established, then any inexplicable noise or flitting shadow is likely to be interpreted by some people in terms of the supernatural rather than simply the unexplained, which is, of course, an entirely different thing.

Empty or derelict houses are particularly likely to attract stories of ghosts, as Owen Davies succinctly puts it, the haunting of such buildings tells us:

> ...what abandonment of a social space meant to the community outside. If people failed to occupy a human environment then external forces would move in; perhaps a mysterious gang of criminals, but maybe also supernatural visitants such as witches, boggarts and ghosts.

It is in such beliefs that we should look for the origins of the majority of haunted house stories, before entering into speculation about theories of residual "psychic" energy left behind by the strong emotions of people after their death.

Chapter 11

Phantom Vehicles and Haunted Roads

Modern accounts of haunted roads generally involve two types of phenomenon—apparitions of people, and apparitions of vehicles. The ghosts of people, often seen on dark roads at night, sometimes border on the "Phantom Hitchhiker" category, discussed in Chapter 8, or they may be a ghost who, for some reason, is confined to a particular stretch of road. Another type of road ghost is the "vanishing victim," where a driver runs into someone with their car, only to discover afterward that the "victim" of the accident has vanished. The main characteristic of phantom vehicles is their sudden inexplicable appearance or disappearance in front of the witness. On some occasions, the model of the car may appear to be of vintage type, and such accounts are closely connected to stories of spectral coaches, common in the 18th and 19th centuries. Reports of phantom vehicles and haunted roads are often connected with fatal car crashes, accidents, or more rarely, murders. However, many accounts, especially of ghost cars, are urban legends if not outright hoaxes, as is evidenced in the fashion of filming staged sightings of "ghost cars," and showing the results on video-sharing Websites such as YouTube.

As has been mentioned previously, ghostly cars and trucks would appear to be direct descendents of the phantom coaches of past ages, but when did the transition from the old fashioned to the modern take place? The change in vehicle type often depends on the place from which the reports originate. Writing in the *California Folklore Quarterly* for April 1942, Rosalie Hankey describes reports of a ghostly coachman at a concrete bridge in Washington, D.C., which stood at the site of the older Rock Creek Bridge, destroyed during a severe storm in 1814. During the collapse, the bridge dragged a coach and its driver into the swirling Potomac River, and there is now "a persistent legend that on nights of bitter storms a ghostly coach and driver can be seen on this bridge, re-enacting this old tragedy." In support of the antique nature of phantom vehicles in some areas at this time, Louis C. Jones writing on New York ghosts in *The Journal of American Folklore* (October–December, 1944), notes that "the ghostly conveyances are almost always old fashioned. We have no record in New York State of a ghostly plane or automobile…"

Reports of such old fashioned vehicles continued to be made well into the 20th century in the United Kingdom, as can be seen in the stories of headless coachmen and coaches dating back to the 1940s, which were included in Anne Bradford's *Worcestershire Ghosts and Hauntings* (2001). However, in the canon of ghost lore such ancient phantoms were rapidly being replaced by more modern vehicular ghosts as the 20th century progressed. Even as far back as the 1930s there were reports from North Kensington of a phantom London bus, which appeared between the Cambridge Gardens and Chesterton Road junctions on St. Mark's Road. Sightings of the ghost bus were always made at the same time, 1:15 a.m. One witness reported: "I was turning the corner and saw a bus tearing towards me, the lights of the top and bottom decks and the headlights were full on but I could not see no crew or passengers." The phantom No. 7 bus was thought to have caused the death of a young motorist in June 1934, when his car unaccountably spun off the road and hit a lamppost at the junction of St. Mark's Road and Cambridge Gardens. Apparently, the bus was to blame for several subsequent crashes at the same spot, before the road was straightened and the phantom was never seen again.

In a recent (2006) magazine survey of the United Kingdom's most haunted highways, the M6, Britain's longest motorway, which runs from near Rugby in the Midlands up to the Scottish border, came out on top with reports of such diverse spirits as phantom monks, spectral Roman soldiers, and ghostly lorries. In the United States, the area in and around Bachelor's Grove cemetery in Chicago is allegedly rife with phantom vehicles. The best time to witness these various ghostly cars and trucks, which are said to appear and disappear on or near the Midlothian Turnpike, which runs past the cemetery, is at dusk or during the evening. One particular report comes from a couple who claimed to have crashed into another vehicle along the turnpike, and described hearing the sound of crushing metal and breaking glass, though the phantom car disappeared before their eyes and left no trace on the road. Another allegedly haunted road in the United States is Clinton Road, in West Milford, New Jersey. According to *Weird New Jersey* magazine the area around this particular road is brimming with ghosts and strange creatures, as well as "gatherings of witches, Satanists and the Ku Klux Klan." Because few, if any, of the reports appear to have been properly investigated, how many of them are urban legends, media generated hoaxes, or tall tales is anyone's guess.

Stories of phantom vehicles are by no means confined to the United States and the United Kingdom. Port Elizabeth highway, which runs between the Hex River Mountains and Drakensberg in the Western Cape province of South Africa, is haunted by a ghostly automobile, which appears to date from the 1960s. The ghost car is said to have caused a number of fatal car accidents during the last decade or so on this particular stretch of the highway. In Georgetown, Penang, Malaysia, there is a particularly notorious T-junction known as "The Deadly Junction," located next to the Union High School. It is believed that anyone who drives in this area late at night will lose control of their car and crash. It is said that the many serious accidents that have occurred at the T-Junction through the years have made it a fatal spot. The evil reputation of the place is also linked to a small tree beside the road, which resembles a woman carrying a child. This woman was apparently a bomoh (shaman/witch doctor) who kidnapped her sister's son and was only seen again on this part of the road.

"J Schotanuswei," a road that connects the villages of Rijs and Oudemirdum in the Netherlands, is frequented by a ghastly apparition that materializes from a hollow tree alongside the road, and also by another less ghoulish apparition known as "the White Woman of the Cellars." The latter ghost has appeared to people lost in snowstorms and helped them find their way home. Another nearby haunted spot is a three-forked road known as "the Boegen," which is haunted by a poltergeist-like entity who delights in playing tricks on local farmers and anyone else unfortunate enough to be passing by. Another road, behind the village of Nijemirdum (to the east of Oudemirdum) is haunted by a large dog with a ring of keys dangling from its neck. In classic black dog fashion (see Chapter 9) this spectre follows travelers for the length of the road, before disappearing without a trace. The Cali Buena Ventura highway, which passes through the Cordillera Occidental Mountains, one of three branches of the Andes Mountains in Colombia, is haunted by an apparition of a short man who is occasionally seen walking along the shoulder. In a version of the Phantom Hitchhiker motif, some drivers who have stopped and offered the mysterious, silent individual a ride have witnessed him suddenly disappear from the seat next to them. One theory is that the figure is the ghost of a native Columbian employed on the Alto Anchicaya Dam, who fell to his death during construction work.

A classic "vanishing victim" story is described in Anne Bradford and Barrie Roberts's *Midland Spirits and Spectres* (1998). The incident occurred on a dark night in 1949, along the A435 opposite Coughton Court in Warwickshire, the magnificent 16th-century home of the Throckmorton family. As a man and his son were driving their Austin 7 past a small lane which runs by the side of Coughton Court, a woman wearing a white mackintosh and riding a bicycle suddenly emerged from the side road and crashed directly into the car. There was no sound, and when the men stopped the car to see what had happened, there was nothing on the road. Bewildered at their experience they knocked on the door of a nearby cottage only to be told that dozens of drivers had reported hitting the phantom cyclist in exactly the same spot.

According to M.A. Richardson, writing in 1842, the next incident occurred around the end of the 18th century, near the village of Tudhoe, County Durham, in the northeast of England. It was almost dusk as the occupier of Tudhoe mill was returning home from Durham where he had been on business. When the miller reached Sunderland Bridge he spotted a man wearing a wide-brimmed hat walking about 20 yards in front of him. Curiously, although the road was straight, he had not noticed the man before.

Desiring some company as night approached, the miller quickened his pace in order to catch up with the stranger, only to find that no matter how fast he walked the man always remained the same distance ahead of him. When they reached "Nicky-nack Bridge" the miller took his eye off the mysterious stranger for a minute and when he looked back he had vanished. There was no where the stranger could have gone and the miller was mystified at the experience.

There is another strange element to this story. A number of years before this sighting, a group of farmers had gathered at a farmer's house in Tudhoe for a harvest feast (known as a "Mell Supper"). After a while, the alcohol ran out, so the farmers sent a mentally retarded laborer out to fetch some more from the nearest public house at Sunderland Bridge. When the man had not returned after three hours, one of the assembled farmers decided to play a trick and frighten him for his lateness. Dressing up in a white sheet the farmer made his way to "Nicky-nack field" and pounced on the young laborer, who ran away as fast as he could, arriving back at the house shaking with fear just as dawn was breaking. When the assembled group asked the simpleton if he had seen anything strange, he answered "Yes, I saw a white ghost which came out and frightened me much, but I saw a black one behind it, so I cried, 'Black ghost catch white ghost.'" At this, the simpleton saw the white ghost look behind him and scream in terror at the site of the black specter. The white ghost tried to run away, but it was too late and it was soon caught by the dark phantom and the two flew away together. Later that day the farmers went out and searched "Nicky-nack field" for their friend but all they were able to find were a few shredded remnants of a white sheet. The farmer who had played the joke was never seen again. This first element of this tale is almost identical to another told about a 17th-century witch known as Meg of Meldon in the neighboring county of

Northumberland. This commonality suggests an origin in folk-lore for both stories, though there are many recorded instances in England from the 16th century onward of practical jokers dressing up in white sheets to frighten travelers on lonely roads at night.

Another similar tale of a strange man on a lonely road was reported to the English Society for Psychical Research (SPR) and first published in their journal in November 1893. The first of a number of sightings during a 10-year period was made by a Miss M.W. Scott, who subsequently wrote to the SPR about it. The date was May 7, 1892, and Miss Scott was returning home after a walk along a road close to the village of St. Boswells, in the Scottish Borders. In somewhat of a hurry, Miss Scott decided to run the rest of the way home but she had not gone far when she...

> ...came to a sudden halt, for just a few yards beyond I perceived a tall man dressed in black, and who walked along at a moderate pace. Fancying he would think mine an extraordinary proceeding, I finally stopped altogether to permit of his getting on further, while at the same time watching him turn the corner and pass on where his figure was still distinctly defined between the hedges...He was gone in a second—there being no exit anywhere—without my having become aware of it...

When reaching the point at which the man vanished Miss Scott encountered her sister, who had also seen the phantom walker, whom she believed to be dressed like an 18th-century clergyman. Miss Scott encountered the strange clergyman again on Sunday June 12th, and this time decided to pursue the man in order to get a closer look at him, only to find that "though he was apparently walking slowly, I never could get any closer than within a few yards, for in a moment he seemed to *float* or skim away." Discussing the case in his *Hauntings and Apparitions* (1982) Andrew Mackenzie mentions other sightings of the ghostly clergyman in the area, and also that Miss Scott had heard locally that "the ghost is believed to be that of a clergyman in St. Boswell's who murdered his servant." On one occasion, Miss Scott described the apparition as wearing a "low crowned hat" with the brim "slouched over his eyes," a similar detail to the Tudhoe phantom, which the miller described as wearing a wide brimmed hat. Indeed, the similarities between the story of the phantom clergyman in black and that from Tudhoe are uncanny. Whatever the origin of these stories, it should be noted that traditionally such darkly dressed apparitions were often associated in popular lore with the Devil.

Almost unique in the annals of ghost lore is the story of the "Hairy Hands" from a desolate stretch of road in Dartmoor, Devon, in the southwest of England. In 1921, a Dr. E.H. Helby, the medical officer for Dartmoor Prison was driving with the two young daughters of the Deputy Governor of the prison on his motorcycle and side car along the road from above Postbridge to Two Bridges. Somewhere along the road, now the B3212, Dr. Helby lost control of his motorbike and crashed. The two children were thrown clear of the sidecar, but the doctor was killed in the accident. Some weeks later a coach driver also lost control of his vehicle on the same stretch of road and several of his passengers were injured. There were other incidents reported from the same part of the road (the hill going into Postbridge) soon after. Two of these involved riders on motorcycles who said that they had felt their hands gripped by invisible "hairy hands," which had tried to throw them off their machines. One of these incidents occurred on August 26, 1921, and involved an army captain, after which the stories were picked up by the *Daily Mail* newspaper and the fame of the "Hairy Hands" went nationwide. After the publicity, there were various theories put forward to explain the phantom hands. Perhaps it was the ghost of the victim of a fatal accident in the area, or even some kind of evil prehistoric "thought form," resentful of the intrusion of modern vehicles into such a peaceful and remote area. After investigations into the road were carried out, however, it was believed that the cause of the accidents was a combination of the dangerous camber of the road and people unfamiliar with the area driving too fast. The road was subsequently altered, and there have apparently been no reports of the "Hairy Hands" since.

As can be seen from the examples of road phantoms in this chapter, many incidents are reported from dangerous junctions or difficult spots on the road. In other words, ideal places for accidents. Indeed it seems to be that one function of ghostly vehicles or human phantoms on roads is to memorialize a place where a fatal accident took place, either in legend or reality. The details of the incident may be forgotten, but there is a memory that "something" unusual took place at the spot. Another function of this type of phantom may be, as Owen Davies has pointed out, to indicate liminality, the border between two states of existence or between the man-made and the natural. Many roads in England lie on Parish boundaries, the origin of which date back to Anglo-Saxon Charters (documents dating from the 7th to the 11th centuries AD). Many parish boundaries include prehistoric monuments such as burial mounds, earthworks, and trackways, and it is possible that some road hauntings still contain elements from folk tales originally associated with these ancient structures that later became attached to roads which followed a similar route. If so, this would make some of our road ghosts very old indeed.

Chapter 12

Time Slips and Spectral Buildings

The so-called "time slip" is a phenomenon where a person or persons witnesses scenes or objects apparently from another time period, predominantly the past. Time slips are often cited as examples of a type of "paranormal" phenomenon known as retrocognition (the ability to see into the past). Another theory is that the witness who experiences a time slip somehow travels back to an earlier time period, or even that past events or objects are projected forward in time. Ghost stories of time slips fall into two categories, either the apparent replaying of past scenes involving modern witnesses, such as the Versailles case, or the appearance of a house, hotel, or cottage from a bygone era, as in the cases of the "Vanishing Hotel" and the phantom house at Rougham Green. Unlike the majority of ghostly tales there are relatively few stories in folklore which relate to the time slip theme, though one or two stories, the Vanishing Hotel Room being one example, are undoubtedly urban legends or modern folk tales.

The most famous and controversial of time slip incident is unquestionably that experienced by Miss Charlotte Moberley (1846–1937) and Miss Eleanor Jourdain (1863–1924), the principal and vice-principal of St. Hugh's College, Oxford. One August afternoon in 1901 the two English academics were visiting the Palace at Versailles, now located in a suburb of Paris, and decided to go and look for the Petit Trianon (a small château located in the grounds of the Palace). While wandering around the grounds both ladies felt a strange sense of oppression in the atmosphere, and encountered a number of people dressed in late 18th-century clothes, as well as landscape and architecture which they later believed to have been present in the park in 1789 (the year that the mobs of the French Revolution stormed Versailles), rather than the early 20th century. Subsequent research into the period of the French Revolution persuaded the ladies that they had somehow slipped back in time to 1789 and met with members of the court of Marie Antoinette (1755–1793), as well as encountered the legendary French Queen herself. Moberley and Jourdain subsequently published their experience in a book called *An Adventure* (1911), under the pseudonyms Elizabeth Morison and Frances Lamont. Ever since the publication of *An Adventure* there has been continuing debate about the strange incident at Versailles, mainly based on the enigma of how the ladies could have learned the details and layout of Versailles in the year 1789 without any prior knowledge of the history of the area.

One down-to-earth explanation for what the English ladies saw was put forward by French author Philippe Jullian in his 1965 book *Prince of Aesthetes: Count Robert De Montesquiou 1855–1892*. Jullian wrote that Moberley and Jourdain had probably chanced upon French aristocrat and poet Comte Robert de Montesquiou-Fezenzac, who was living at Versailles around the time of their visit. Montesquiou sometimes held fancy dress parties in the grounds at Versailles, where he and his friends would dress in period costumes and perform *tableaux vivants* ("living pictures"), where they re-enacted paintings, sculptures, and historical scenes. It is indeed possible that such parties involving the French decadent avant-garde of the period could answer the descriptions given by the two English dons, and may also have made a somewhat disturbing impression on them. However, tempting as it is to accept Philippe Jullian's "theatrical production" explanation for what the women experienced, it still leaves the matter of the different scenery they claimed to have seen unaccounted for. It has also never been proven for certain that Montesquiou and his friends were at Versailles the same day on which Moberley and Jourdain were visiting. There have also been other reports of time slips at Versailles, though as these incidents have not been thoroughly investigated and documented it is difficult to judge their validity.

Critics of the Versailles case, including W.H. Salter of the Society for Psychical Research, have noted that much of the material about the experience that Moberley and Jourdain supposedly recorded in 1901 was in fact written down much later, in 1906, after they had researched the history of Versailles. This is an important point, as the ladies were supposedly ignorant of the details of French Revolution-period Versailles in 1901, so they would not have been able to give accurate descriptions of it. But if Moberley and Jourdain later added historical details to their original account to make it more realistic, does it mean that nothing unusual happened to them on that August day in 1901? It certainly seems unlikely that two respected academics would have invented the story, though it is possible that while walking around the grounds of Versailles, perhaps suffering from overtiredness at being lost, historical events that they had read or heard about produced a "bygone Versailles" in their mind's eye. It should also be noted that Eleanor Jourdain also claimed to have had numerous "psychic visions" of scenes from the past in Oxford in 1902. Whatever the explanation, to the end of their days the two women sincerely believed they experienced something out of the ordinary on their visit to Versailles in 1901.

Another fascinating case, this time concerning a phantom house, also involved two women and was reported to Sir Ernest Bennett who published it in his book *Apparitions and Haunted Houses* (1938). The incident occurred in October 1926, near Bury St. Edmunds, in Suffolk, England. School teacher Ruth Wynne had recently arrived in the area and wanting to explore, took her 14-year-old pupil, a Miss Allington, for a walk from Rougham Green rectory toward Bradfield St. George church. It was an overcast afternoon and as the women were walking through a farmyard toward the road they noticed, exactly opposite them, a high brick wall with iron gates through which they saw a large Georgian house peeping out from behind a cluster of tall trees. Miss Wynne was rather surprised that no one had mentioned the house and its owners, but thinking nothing more of it the pair carried along the footpath to the church, which was only about 300 feet away. The women returned home via a short cut, which did not pass the house. It was not until the following year, in February or March, that Ruth Wynne and her pupil took the same walk again, but when they walked through the farm yard and out onto the road they found to their astonishment that there was no wall, gates, or house. Instead the area was covered with a mass of overgrown trees, mounds, weeds, and ponds. The women never saw the house again, and subsequent research has found no record of a Georgian mansion existing in the area. No one has ever come up with a satisfactory explanation for what the two women might have seen, though it is always a possibility that, being new to the area, they simply lost their way and were mistaken about the location of the house.

Another account of a phantom house in the same area was published in the magazine *Amateur Gardening* for December 20, 1975, by someone writing under the pseudonym of "James Cobbold." The article described the house, which Cobbold said he saw in June 1911 or 1912, as a three-story Georgian red brick. The author also claimed that he witnessed the house vanish as he was looking at it—"a kind of mist seemed to envelope the house, which I could still see, and the whole thing simply disappeared, it just went." The location of this ghostly building was not the same as the one seen by Ruth Wynne and Miss Allington, and the account does sound a little far-fetched, perhaps being inspired by Ruth Wynne's original story.

A much more controversial tale, where the witnesses claimed to have interacted with people apparently from a bygone age, came to public attention when it was featured in the United Kingdom TV show *Strange But True* in 1979. In October 1979, two English married couples, the Simpsons and the Gisbys, went on a driving holiday together, which was to take them through France and Spain. The couples claimed that they stayed at a curiously old-fashioned small hotel, in the Rhone Valley near Montelimar, in southern France. There were no modern conveniences such as telephones, TVs, or elevators at the hotel and in place of locks on the doors there were wooden latches. The beds had no pillows and there was no glass in the windows, only wooden shutters. When they paid the bill the next day the couples were amazed to find that they were only charged a few francs for the night's lodgings and the meals they had eaten. The staff of the hotel and the local gendarmes also seemed to be wearing very old-fashioned clothes. On their way back from two weeks in Spain, the couples decided to stay at the odd little hotel again, but although they drove down the same streets as before, they were unable to find the hotel. When thy returned to England the Simpsons and the Gisbys had their rolls of film from the holiday developed only to find that the pictures taken at the hotel had vanished. This is a bizarre but suspicious case, mainly because it is difficult to believe that the hotel manager, the staff, and the gendarmes whom the couples met would have shown no reaction whatsoever to such a futuristic (for them) vehicle as a modern car, nor to their 1970s French currency.

This spectral building story has many elements in common with a well-known urban legend called The Vanishing Hotel room, some versions of which are also set in France. Briefly, the most popular account of the Vanishing Hotel legend involves an English woman who is traveling back from India with her daughter and falls ill while staying at a hotel in Paris. The daughter leaves her mother in bed and heads out across Paris to pick up a prescription for the medicine her mother needs. When the daughter finally returns to the hotel after hours of searching for the medicine she finds that no-one there recognizes her and that both her mother and the room they had stayed in have vanished. In one ending of the story the girl never sees her mother again nor finds out what happened to her. In another version of the tale the daughter doggedly investigates the disappearance until she discovers that her mother had contracted the plague (or some other deadly disease), which the doctor had diagnosed and consequently had her moved from the hotel to the hospital where she had died. Fearful of losing tourist revenue the hotel management had the room completely redecorated and the incident was hushed up to avoid panic. Variations of this story, often cited as a true incident in many books on the "unexplained," have been in circulation for at least a century, and if nothing else show the dangers of accepting supernatural "true" stories at face value.

An even closer parallel with the Simpson/Gisby case, as well as the Bury St. Edmunds tale can be found in Louis C. Jones article "The Ghosts of New York: An Analytical Study" in *The Journal of*

American Folklore for October–December 1944. This folk story described by Jones concerns two travelers who spent a night at a house owned by a particularly pleasant couple:

> Because the hosts were poor the travellers left a fifty-cent piece on a marbletop table when they departed early in the morning. In the next town people told them there was no such house any more, nor any such people as they described—though all admitted that there had been, long before, such a couple, now dead and buried, and such a house, now a heap of rubble and ashes. So the perplexed travellers returned to find the driveway overgrown, and only a gaping cellar full of burned timbers and refuse. One curious item they did locate-the cracked and sooty marble top of what had once been a handsome table. On top of the dust was shining a fifty-cent piece.

Dartmoor, an area of bleak moorland in southwest England, seems to have its very own "phantom cottage" seen by a number of witnesses at various locations in the area through the years. Some time in the first half of the 20th century, a party of three girls were on a shooting expedition with their father near the small town of Buckfastleigh, an area of Dartmoor steeped in ghost lore. During the hunt the girls were separated from their father and became lost due to the darkness. Eventually, they saw a light ahead of them, which they ran toward to find a cottage by the road, lit up from the inside by firelight. Looking through the window the girls saw an old man and woman sitting by the fire, but as they were watching the entire scene suddenly disappeared and the girls were once again alone in the darkness. In his book, *Haunted Britain* (1948), Elliot O'Donnell recounts one of the many phantom house stories told to him through the years. This tale involved a lady and her friend who were staying in the town of Chagford, on the northeastern edge of Dartmoor, and decided to go for a walk across the moor one summer afternoon. After rambling around for a few hours, the ladies arrived at two picturesque cottages, which made such an impression on them that they knocked on the door of one of them to inquire if there were any apartments available. The door was answered by a pretty little fair-haired girl who asked them to wait while she fetched her mother. While waiting, the two women noticed the distinctly old world style of decoration in the cottage and a strange looking black bird in a cage. The mother soon arrived, a tall, dark attractive woman with an enigmatic far away look in her eyes, who told them that there were presently no rooms available. As often seems the case in these phantom house stories, the two women were not in the area again until the following year, when they again went in search of the cottages. However, the ladies were unable to locate the buildings, though they found the spot in which they thought the cottages had stood. On further enquiry the two women found that no such cottages had ever existed in the vicinity, and that they must have seen Dartmoor's Phantom Cottages, said to appear on the moor every 10 or 12 years.

Another of Dartmoor's ghostly cottages is described by Ruth E. St. Leger-Gordon in *Witchcraft and Folklore of Dartmoor* (1966). This time the cottage appeared closed to the village of Islington, on the east side of Dartmoor, in the early 1960s and was witnessed on two separate occasions by a visitor to the area and an Ordnance Surveyor. The landowner, who was born on the estate where the cottage was seen, was adamant that no such cottage had ever existed in the area.

It may be thought from reading the previous accounts (most of which date from between 1900 and 1965) that time slips and spectral buildings are no longer reported. However, in the 1990s there were various accounts of apparent time slips from Bold Street in the center of Liverpool. A number of witnesses, including an off duty policeman, reported being transported back in time along this road, finding themselves on a cobbled street with old-fashioned shops and people dressed in 1940s clothing.

A number of explanations have been put forward for time slips and spectral buildings from the past. Could the witnesses to the strange phenomena have been transported back in time, or been fortunately present when some kind of window on the past opened up allowing the observer to see through it? While interesting, such physics-defying explanations do not really clarify anything. Because they are unproven and entirely speculative theories they complicate the mystery rather than add anything to our understanding of it. For the majority of the phantom building stories the most obvious explanation is that the witnesses became disoriented and confused about their location, which was, in the majority of cases, an area entirely unfamiliar to them. Other cases, such as the Vanishing Hotel, would seem to be more akin to urban legend than actual experience. Time Slips like the Bold Street examples are more complicated. The evidence suggests that perhaps only certain types of people experience the phenomenon. Eleanor Jourdain, for example, seems to have been particularly prone to such "visions." If this is the case then a time slip may be something that occurs not in physical reality, but entirely within the mind of individuals who are easily impressed by certain outside stimuli, which bring about a sudden change in their consciousness. On the surface of it, this explanation would not seem to apply to cases like that at Versailles, which involves a pair of witnesses. Nevertheless, the details of many of these experiences, especially the older ones, are sketchy, and more detailed investigation of existing records would need to be carried out to discover if the stories of each of the individual witnesses in the cases did, in fact, agree.

Chapter 13

Screaming Skulls

A "Screaming Skull" is a human skull of uncertain origin which is or was kept in a number of English farms and manor houses, usually on display in a prominent position. The Screaming Skull tradition seems for some reason to be confined entirely to England, and in their 1996 study in *Fortean Studies* Andy Roberts and David Clarke identified 27 examples from the country. The object is generally regarded as a talisman by its owners, bringing luck and protection to the family as long as it remains in the house. There is usually a traditional tale to explain how the skull came to be in the house, and how, when the object was removed from its original place, all hell broke loose—there were terrible storms, wild screams, outbreaks of fire, poltergeist-type activity, and even death. The only way to restore peace in the home was to put the skull back in its proper place. What is the origin of such a unique and interesting type of haunting, and is there any truth behind the many strange tales concerning these "Screaming Skulls"?

Bettiscombe Manor, until recently the ancestral home of the Pinney family, is located in the village of Bettiscombe, near Bridport, in Dorset, southwest England. The manor was constructed in 1694 on the site of an Elizabethan house, though the first mention of the existence of a Screaming Skull there is not until 1847 by Mrs. Anna Pinney, when it was being kept on a beam in the attic near a main chimney. Mrs. Pinney was told that the macabre object brought good luck "and while this skull is kept, no ghost will ever invade Bettiscombe." A niche was later constructed for the skull in the attic, but by the 1980s the strange relic was housed in a cardboard shoebox in the study, still, however, close to a chimney. In their weighty tome of English folklore, *The Lore of the Land,* Jennifer Westwood and Jacqueline Simpson note that at all times the skull seems to have been kept near a chimney. This fact ties in well with the tradition of hiding magical protective objects in the brickwork of a chimney or in the roof space of a building, thus guarding the parts of the house most vulnerable to supernatural attack.

The Bettiscombe Manor Screaming Skull, the first to be given that appellation, probably some time in the late Victorian period, has accumulated a considerable amount of ghost lore around it. One tale is set in the 1740s and involves John Frederick Pinney (or in other versions his grandfather Azariah Pinney) who lived at Bettiscombe Manor, but later inherited a large sugar plantation on the island of Nevis in the West Indies. Apparently disgusted at the slave trade, Pinney returned to Dorset bringing a male slave with him as his servant to live at Bettiscombe. In one of the many variations of this story, it is the dying wish of the African servant that his body be returned to his native land for burial. However, for whatever reason, the man's wish is ignored, and he is instead buried in the local churchyard. Almost immediately local villagers began to complain of terrible screams coming from the direction of the grave, and various poltergeist-like phenomena also plagued the house. The body was subsequently exhumed and decapitated, the head being placed in the attic of Bettiscombe with the instructions that it should never be moved. Apparently after this was done there were no more ghostly disturbances in the house. According to another tale this Screaming Skull lets out a terrifying scream whenever it is removed from the house. On one occasion a tenant at Bettiscombe is said to have tried to get rid of the grisly relic by throwing it into a pond. However, such were the noises and screams within the house that he was forced to return a few days later to retrieve the skull and put it back in its original position.

The majority of the colorful tales which surround the Screaming Skull of Bettiscombe can be traced back to a Dorset antiquarian named J.S. Udal, who wrote to the journal *Notes and Queries* about the object in 1872. Udal, who had been told the stories of the skull by an 80-year-old woman who had often stayed at Bettiscombe in her youth, stated that it had been kept in its place because people believed that

> ...if it be brought out of the house, the house itself would rock to its foundation, whilst the person by whom such an act of desecration was committed would certainly die within the year.

Even as late as the 1960s one farm worker claimed that he would hear the skull "screaming like a trapped rat in the attic." In the 1880s Udal examined the skull and was of the opinion that it was that of a woman rather than a man. This fact was confirmed when the Pinney family had the object tested by a pathologist in 1963, who also estimated that the skull was 3,000 to 4,000 years old. The patina of the skull indicates that it may have been immersed in water with a high mineral content, perhaps the well near the manor house, and could, considering its date, originate from the Iron Age hillfort of Pilsdon Pen, which overlooks the well.

The magnificent 400-year-old Burton Agnes Hall, in the East Riding of Yorkshire, is also home to a Screaming Skull. In her 1912 book, *East Riding of Yorkshire*, Eliza Gutch records the story surrounding the skull, using information from local periodical *Yorkshire Chat*. The tale quoted by Gutch reports that three sisters of the Griffiths family were living in an old Norman manor house near the village church, waiting for the completion of their new house. On one particular occasion, one of the sisters, Miss Anne, was out walking in the park when she was fatally wounded by an outlaw in a botched robbery attempt. Before her death Anne made her two sisters promise that a part of her would forever remain within the walls of their beautiful future home, which she never lived to see completed:

> This they agreed to do, but after her death they buried her without fulfilling the compact. Nothing happened until they took up their abode at Burton Agnes. Then strange moanings and weird sounds made the sisters' lives a burden to them. No servants would stay; so at last after two years they caused the body to be dug up and decapitated, and placed the now fleshless head upon the table.

In *The Haunted Homes and Family Traditions of Great Britain*, first published in the 1880s, John H. Ingram gives some more detail to the legends of Burton Agnes. According to Ingram, who quotes an article from the *Leeds Mercury* by F. Ross, the three ladies lived in the Elizabethan period (1558–1603) and were co-heiresses of the Burton Agnes Estate. After the skull of Anne Griffiths was brought into the house many attempts were made to get rid of it, but all were unsuccessful. No sooner had the skull been taken away than ghostly knockings would begin all over the house, and the occupants of Burton Agnes would have no peace until it was returned. According to Ross (quoted by Ingram):

> On one occasion a maid-servant threw it from the window upon a passing load of manure, but from that moment the horses were not able to move the waggon an inch, and despite the vigorous whipping of the waggoner, all their efforts were in vain, until the servant confessed what she had done, when the skull was brought back into the house, and the horses drew the waggon along without the least difficulty.

In the 19th century the servants of the family would refer to Anne's ghost as "Awd Nance," and it is said that even today the Queen's State Bedroom at the hall is haunted by Anne, in the form of "the blue lady." There is also a tradition that at some time in the past the Boynton family, who inherited the hall in 1654 and believed in the talismanic qualities of the skull, had a niche built in the wall and the object bricked up inside. The exact location of Anne's skull (if that is who it belonged to), safely hidden behind paneling in one of the many bedrooms, is now only known to the family and members of staff at Burton Agnes Hall.

Wardley Hall, near Manchester, is one of the few buildings in the northwest of England mentioned in the Domesday Book, one of Britain's earliest surviving public records, completed in 1086. The present building dates from the 16th century and is currently the home of the Roman Catholic Bishop of Salford. Wardley Hall is known as "The House of the Skull" due to the human skull kept in a glass fronted aperture over the main staircase. There are various curious traditions associated with the skull, some of which were described by Manchester antiquary Thomas Barritt, who visited the hall in 1782. John H. Ingram quotes Barritt:

> A human skull which, time out of mind, hath had a superstitious veneration paid to it by [the occupiers of the Hall] not permitting it to be removed from its situation, which is on the topmost step of a staircase. There is a tradition that, if removed or ill-used, some uncommon noise and disturbance always follows, to the terror of the whole house...some years ago, I and three of my acquaintances went to view this surprising piece of household furniture...one of us...removed it from its place into a dark part of the room, and then left, and returned home; but the night but one following, such a storm arose about the house, of wind and lightening, as tore down some trees, and unthatched out-housing...

Barritt learned a strange story from some older residents of the neighborhood as to the skull being that of Roger Downes, the last male heir of the family occupying the Hall in the 17th century:

> ...a young man of the Downes family, being in London, one night in his frolics vowed to his companions that he would kill the first man he met; and accordingly he ran his sword through a man immediately, a tailor by trade. However, justice overtook him in his career of wickedness; for in some while after, he being in a riot upon London Bridge, a watchman made a stroke at him with his bill, and severed his head from his body, which head was enclosed in a box, and sent to his sister, who then lived at Wardley, where it hath continued ever since.

However, this story was proved to be fiction when, in 1799, Roger Downes's coffin was located inside the family vault, and, when opened, his skeleton was found to be complete. The most likely candidate for the skull seems to be the martyr Father Ambrose Barlow, hung, drawn, and quartered for his faith in 1641, and canonized in 1970. After his execution, Barlow's head was displayed on a spike on the tower of Manchester's old church. According to some sources, the head was brought by Catholic sympathizers to Wardley, where it was kept as a religious relic, hidden in the wall of the chapel by the Downes, Catholics, and friends of Ambrose Barlow's family.

Higher Farm, a 17th-century Georgian farmhouse in the quiet village of Chilton Cantelo, Somerset, contains a Screaming Skull displayed on a high cabinet shelf in the hall, facing the main entrance to the property. The skull is believed to be that of Theophilus Broome, who died in 1670 and whose body was buried in St. James's Church in the village. The story of Broome's head being preserved at the farm was first recorded in 1791 by John Collinson in his *History and Antiquities of Somerset*, who describes it thus:

> There is a tradition in this parish that the person here interred requested that his head might be taken off before his burial and be preserved at the farmhouse near the church, where a head, chop-fallen enough, is still shown, which the tenants of the house have often endeavoured to commit to the bowels of the earth, but have as often been deterred by horrid noises portentive of sad displeasure; and about twenty years since (which was perhaps the last attempt) the sexton, in digging the place for the skull's repository, broke the spade in two pieces, and uttered a solemn asseveration never more to attempt an act so evidently repugnant to the quiet of Brome's Head.

Local tradition asserts that Broome had fought in the English Civil War on the side of the Parliamentarians and was terrified at the Royalist practice of posthumously beheading the corpses of Republican sympathizers and displaying them on spikes (see Chapter 4 for more on this practice). Not wanting his body treated in this demeaning fashion, Broome desired that his head was to be hidden at the farmhouse where he had once lived. In support of this tale, in the mid-19th-century it is said that Broome's grave was opened and his skeleton was indeed found to be headless.

Various theories have been put forward to explain the Screaming Skull tradition in England. One hypothesis is that the preservation of these severed heads is a continuation of a pre-Christian Celtic head cult, such as is suggested by finds of numerous skulls from Celtic Iron Age sites like Bredon Hill in Worcestershire. Celtic myth and folklore also includes various tales connected with severed heads, most importantly that of the giant and king Bran the Blessed, whose dying wish is that his head be cut off and buried on the White Hill (perhaps the site of the Tower) in London. The Celtic theory is interesting, though one wonders why there are no tales of Screaming Skulls from more traditionally Celtic areas such as Wales, Ireland, Scotland, and Brittany. There is also a huge time lag between the Celtic Iron Age (roughly 600 BC to AD 50 in Britain) and the first appearance of Screaming Skull tales, which is not until the end of the 18th century. More probably the traditions attached to the skulls and their association with talismanic qualities is the result of a combination of factors. Skulls were often used in traditional medicine, water could be drunk from them (in 1826 workmen used the Chilton Cantelo skull to drink beer from), or fragments were grated into food for curative purposes.

The skulls may also have served a similar function as the animal bones occasionally found secreted under floors or bricked up in the chimneys and walls of old houses, most likely as protection against witchcraft or other evil forces. What is certain is that many of the occupants of the houses where these skulls are preserved regarded them as the "luck" of the family, akin to an heirloom, which must be kept safe to preserve the good fortune of the home and the family. As to the origins of the skulls themselves, despite the colorful traditions surrounding them, some were probably dug from prehistoric burial mounds by antiquarians in the 18th or 19th centuries, as seems to be the case with the Bettiscombe example, while others may have belonged to medical students or artists. Some skulls may even have been kept as a *memento mori*, reminders of the owner's own mortality, such as the large silver watch, carved into the form of a human skull that Mary Queen of Scots reputedly had made just before her execution on February 8, 1587.

Chapter 14

Ghostly Lights

Ghostly lights are a world-wide phenomenon found under many different names with varying characteristics. The most common type is usually seen at night or twilight flickering over bogs, swamps, and rivers, and referred to in the Latin as the *ignis fatuus* ("foolish fire"). In folklore this phenomenon is known as the will-o'-the-wisp, Jack-o'-lantern, and many other local names. Variations on the ghostly light or glow include the "corpse candle" of Wales and parts of Scotland, the "treasure lights" of Denmark and other north European countries, the "Gandaspati" of Indonesia, the Min Min Light of Australia, and the various "spook lights" or "ghost lights," such as the Brown Mountain Lights and the Marfa Lights, reported from the United States.

Lore of the Ghost

The mischievous spirit known as the will-o'-the-wisp is common in the folktales and ghost lore of many countries. Though the origins given for this ghostly phenomenon may vary from culture to culture, its characteristics are usually the same, the light suggesting an otherworldly being carrying a burning bundle of straw as a torch to lead the foolish traveler astray. The will-o'-the-wisp was discussed as far back as the 16th century by theologian William Fulke (1536/7–1589), who, in his book *A Goodly Gallerye with a most Pleasaunt Prospect* (London 1563), put forward his own explanation for its cause:

> ...ignorant and superstitious fooles have thought [them] to be soules tormented in the fire of Purgatory...the Devill hath used these lights (although they be naturally caused) as strong delusions to captive the minds of men with feare of the Popes Purgatory...[people] will tell a great tale, how they have beene led about by a spirit in the likeness of Fire.

In one tale from Shropshire in England, quoted by folklorist Katherine Briggs in her *Dictionary of Fairies* (1977), a wicked blacksmith was given a second chance at life by Saint Peter when he arrived at the gates to heaven. However, afterward the smith led a life of such impiety that he was doomed to wander the earth with a single piece of burning coal to warm himself, given to him by the Devil, with which he lured poor travelers to their death over boggy ground. A few tales of a similar kind are found in Donald Ward's *The German Legends of the Brothers Grimm* (1981). One of these is called "The Will-O'-the-Wisp," and describes ghost lights, known as "Heerwische," being reported from Hänlein, (southeast of Darmstadt) on the Mountain Highway, and also to the south in the region of Lorsch. The Heerwische are said to appear during Advent (the period immediately preceding Christmas) and there is a verse traditionally directed at them:

Heerwische! Haw, Haw!
Burn like oat straw!
Strike me Lightning fast!

The cautionary tale quoted by Ward goes on:

> It is said that more than thirty years ago a girl saw a Heerwische, and she taunted it with the rhyme. It flew directly at the girl, who turned and fled home to her parents. But it followed right on her heels into the room. There, it struck everyone present with its fiery wings and they lost both sight and hearing.

Another story from the Grimms, which blends the motif of ghostly lights with that of the sunken city, is The Maidens of the Moors, set in the Rhon Mountains of central Germany. A swamp called the Red Marsh is said to contain the village of Poppenrode, which sank into the ground some time in the remote past. It was believed by locals that at night tiny lights could be seen hovering above the surface of the marsh. Finally, in the The Accursed Surveyors, the Grimms recorded that the strange lights seen at night flitting back and forth around river banks and hedgerows were believed to be the ghosts of land surveyors who cheated when measuring property boundaries. In their afterlife these land surveyors were fated to wander around and keep watch over those same boundaries. In Denmark, according to H.F. Feilberg writing in *Folklore* for September 1895, the will-o'-the-wisp was believed to be the "soul of an unrighteous surveyor, or of an unbaptized, murdered child." The latter belief accords well with the idea found in British folklore that the lights are sometimes believed to be the ghosts of unbaptized or stillborn children, hovering between heaven and hell. If these lights were not seen as ghosts then, in British and Irish folklore especially, they would often be interpreted as a kind of fairy, usually tricksters such as Puck, Robin Goodfellow, or, in

Devon, the pixies. Sometimes the regional name for a ghostly light, like "Hobbledy's lantern" in Warwickshire, Worcestershire, and Gloucestershire for example, gives a clue to its fairy associations.

Writing in the journal *Folklore* for December 1894, M.J. Walhouse describes will-o'-the-wisps, known as "Bhûtni"(from "Bhûta," a goblin) being frequently reported from the flat marshy country under the Rajmahal Hills, to the west of the town of Rajmahal, in the state of Jharkhand, India. The locals' explanation for the lights was that they were carried about by ghosts. Walhouse also discusses a tribe of wizards from Burma:

> ...whose heads are believed to leave their bodies during the night and wander in the jungle feeding on carrion, and the ignis fatuus is said to issue from their mouths; if one of these heads be seized it screams and struggles to escape, and if kept away from the body for more than twelve hours both perish

The Shanars, a caste of Indian merchants and traders today known as the Nadars, believed that burialgrounds were haunted by shape-shifting demons that were frequently witnessed "gliding over marshy land like flickering lights." These ghostly lights were called in Tamil *pey-neruppu* (**"devil-fires"**).

Another function of the will-o'-the-wisp category of ghost lights is to mark the supposed location of treasure buried deep underground or sometimes under water. In Devon, in the south west of England, the Jack-o'-Lantern was believed to glow over places where metal ore deposits lay buried. The treasure tradition, found mainly in northern European countries such as Finland, Sweden, and Denmark, was that during midsummer, said to be the best time to search for these treasure lights, treasure would be found when the lights were seen burning. In Denmark, the lights were witnessed on hills where castles or other ancient ruins were located, though what lay hidden was not always treasure bit could also be an evil deed.

The "Corpse Candle" (*Canwyll Corph* in Welsh) is another type of ghostly light, known mainly from Wales, though there are examples from the border districts of the Highlands of Scotland, and Denmark. In Welsh folk tradition, the corpse candle originated in the fifth century AD with St. David, the patron saint of Wales, who prayed that his people should have some kind of warning to help them prepare for death. Marie Trevelyan in her classic work *Folk-lore and Folk-Stories of Wales* (1909), states that the corpse candle was usually witnessed gliding above ground along the route to be taken by a funeral, or hovering above the area where an accident would happen. According to the lore attached to this particular type of Welsh ghost light, if two corpse candles were seen then two funerals would take place, a tall light warned of the death of a man, a lesser one for a woman, and a small light forewarned the death of a child. The colors of the light also varied, a man's death would be preceded by a red glowing light, a woman's by a pale blue one and a faint, pale yellow light appeared before a child's death. In Denmark, according to H.F. Feilberg in his *Folklore* article: "If a corpse candle be small, but red and bright, it is that of a child; the candle of a grown up man or woman is larger but paler, and that of an aged person is blue." Feilberg also notes that in Denmark if a person is ill his death is forewarned by a light seen at night slowly floating from the house to the gate of the churchyard and along the churchroad, which is usually the route taken by funeral processions.

Tales of the corpse candle from throughout Wales are extremely similar, in fact sometimes the stories are identical and only the location has been changed, a common occurrence in folklore. One of these incidents is said to have taken place in the southwest of Wales in the 18th century:

> In passing Golden Grove from Llandilo to Carmarthen, several people...saw three corpse-candles gliding down the river at various times three weeks in succession. The persons compared

their experiences and wondered what the omen meant. Was it for the villagers or was it for the noble family who lived at Golden Grove? At length the solution came. Three members of the nobleman's family died simultaneously in different parts of the country.

Another story quoted by Trevelyan from the same general area, Disgwilfa, about 12 miles from Carmarthen, describes a strange light "seen glimmering in the corner of a field, where the branches of a tall sycamore-tree made a deep shadow." The light was seen hovering in the same place, a few feet from the field gate, by a number of people for a year before it unaccountably disappeared. The next day a local gentleman out hunting fell from his horse as he was jumping the field gate and was killed, in the very place where the glimmering corpse candle had been seen. Such standing lights seem to be a slight variant on the corpse candle motif, and are also found in Denmark. H.F. Feilberg recounts a tale from the area of his village where a "standing" light was witnessed near a dangerous ford over a large rivulet by many people for generations. The ford was much in use as it saved going a much longer way around. On one occasion, a young farmer was crossing the ford on horseback when the horse lost its footing and the young man was plunged into the water and drowned. Apparently the locals, afraid of what the light portended, had warned the farmer not to use the crossing but he had ignored them.

The most widely accepted explanation for the will-o'-the-wisp is that it is caused by the spontaneous ignition of methane gases produced by the decay of vegetation in marshy or boggy areas. However, not all cases of ghost lights occurred out of doors. An 1804 issue of *The Times* newspaper, quoted by Owen Davies in *The Haunted: A Social History of Ghosts* (2007), reported that a farmhouse built over a disused coal pit around Bilston in the English West Midlands, was being haunted by a fiery spirit light. One evening the serving woman went down to the cellar to dispose of the household waste into an opening there when a blue flame suddenly leapt out of the hole almost driving her out of her wits with fear. When the incident was investigated, however, it was discovered that the ghost light had been caused by an ignition of mine gas.

Many cases of spirit lights were more easily explained, and often turned out to be nothing more than someone with a candle or lantern walking along an alleyway or lane after dark. During lambing time, shepherds moving around the hills at night carrying a lantern were sometimes the cause of such reports. In the *History and Reality of Apparitions* (1727), Daniel Defoe describes a revealing hoax carried out by schoolboys from Dorking, Surry, in the south of England, in the house of an old lady who had recently passed away. One night one of the boys wandered around the house and nearby fields with a lantern, persuading the neighbors that the luminous spirit of the old lady had come back to haunt them.

Japanese folklore has many versions of the ghostly light, the most interesting of which are known as "Hitodama" ("human ball" or "human soul"). These ghostly spheres, pale blue or green in color with spiraling tails, are often believed to be the souls of the newly dead, and are most commonly reported from dark forests in the summer and around graveyards. Hitodama are sometimes thought to originate from luminous gases that can apparently be seen above human graves. Similar to the European will-o'-the-wisp, Hitodama can behave as a trickster, and there are folktales where they lead travelers great distances off their path leaving them lost and alone.

Spook lights are the modern American equivalent of the will-o'-the-wisp and corpse candle of European folklore. The most famous of these spook lights are probably the Brown Mountain Lights of North Carolina, small star-like lights witnessed on Brown Mountain, on the Blue Ridge in the Pisgah National Forest. There is very little genuine folklore attached to these lights, although various Websites claim that there are Native American myths describing the lights as either the spirits of Native Americans who died in battle or the lanterns of Indian maidens searching for those killed while fighting. However, apart from this single Cherokee legend, which may or may not relate to Brown Mountain, there is no documentary proof of anything about the lights in Native American folklore or myth.

The earliest published report of unexplained lights in the area was featured in the *Charlotte Daily Observer* for September 24, 1913. The light, which was seen to rise above the horizon at the same time every night, was described in the *Observer* as red in color and "much like a toy fire balloon." Though the newspaper account dates from 1913, the sighting described was actually made by members of the Morganton Fishing Club in 1908 or 1909. In October 1913, a Mr. Sterrett of the United States. Geological Survey investigated the mysterious lights and concluded that what the Fishing Club members had seen were locomotive headlights. A further U.S. Geological Survey report from 1922 concluded that the Brown Mountain Lights were caused by a variety of manmade sources, including headlights, house lights, and campfires. To this list of possible explanations should be added campers' flashlights and the lights of planes taking off from the Morganton-Lenoir Airport.

The Brown Mountain Lights have become something of a tourist attraction for the area, as have the "Marfa Mystery Lights," which have been reported from the Mitchell Flat area, to the east of Marfa, Texas. The Marfa Lights have been described as brightly glowing soccer or basket ball-size lights floating above the ground, or sometimes high in the air. As with the Brown Mountain Lights folklore relating directly to the Marfa Lights is pretty thin on the gound. One Apache legend, of uncertain date and origin, explains the lights as the spirit of Apache Chief called Alaste, who was allegedly executed at the hands of Mexican Rurales (Rural Guard) in the 1860s. Another version of this unconfirmed legend is that the lights are the campfires of Alaste's tribe who were apparently massacred by the

Mexicans. Recorded sources for the lights are said to stretch back to the mid 19th century, though no documentary proof has ever been produced for these claims. The origin of most of the mystique surrounding the lights can be traced back to an article by Paul Moran, "The Mystery of the Texas Ghost Light," in the July 1957 edition of *Coronet Magazine.* Although there is no doubt that the Marfa Lights exist, recent research into their origin by students from The Society of Physics Students at the University of Texas at Dallas, as well as by independent researcher Bill Welker, has shown that the most likely explanation for the majority of sightings of the Marfa Lights are automobile headlights seen over a great distance.

Australia has its own version of the spook lights of the United States, namely the Min Min Light, which has been reported from places as far apart as Brewarrina in western New South Wales and Boulia in northern Queensland. The Min Min Light is an unexplained formation of blurry disc-shaped lights that appear to hover just above the horizon, and has sometimes been reported as following travelers for considerable distances. Many of the sightings of these bobbing lights have been identified as barn owls flying a foot above the ground while hunting. Another possible explanation was put forward in early 2003 by neuroscientist Professor Jack Pettigrew, of the University of Queensland in Brisbane. Pettigrew's research suggested that the Min Min Light was caused by an inverted mirage of light sources sometimes located hundreds of miles distant over the horizon. Such mirages are known as *Fata Morgana*, after King Arthur's half sister the sorceress Morgan Le Fay, and are caused by temperature inversion. Pettigrew managed to re create the effect which he believes causes the Min Min Light using automobile headlights, and his results were published as "The Min Min light and the Fata Morgana— An optical account of a mysterious Australian phenomenon" in *Clinical and Experimental Optometry* (Vol. 86, pp. 109–120).

Chapter 15

Phantom

Sounds and

Ghostly Aromas

Though ghostly sounds (sometimes known as "audible ghosts") are most closely connected with poltergeist activity, discussed elsewhere in this book, they are also well documented in ghost lore as isolated occurrences. Phantom footsteps, ghostly voices, and otherworldly music have been reported for centuries and continue to be today. Indeed investigations into the supposed voices of the dead in the form of Electronic Voice Phenomena (EVP) is now a study area of its own within the paranormal field. In contrast, curious odors or smells ("olfactory ghosts") are only associated with a relatively small percentage of ghostly incidents. In their 1975 book *Apparitions*, Celia Green and Charles McCreery wrote that only 8 percent of respondents to an appeal by the Institute of Psychophysical

Research reported odors associated with apparitions, in comparison with the 37 percent who reported auditory experiences.

Phantoms who call attention to their presence by such non-visual means are often termed "invisible ghosts," though of course there are a number of cases where there is a visual apparition accompanied by sound or smell. One example that includes smell and sound, as well as other bizarre phenomena more commonly associated with poltergeist activity is quoted in W.B. Yeats's *Fairy and Folk Tales of the Irish Peasantry*, first published in 1888. The incidents that were alleged to have taken place led to the last witch-craft trial recorded in Ireland, in County Antrim, in March 1711. The story goes that a young woman named Mary Dunbar fell into violent fits and claimed she was being tormented by several women, all of whom she named (in the manner of the Salem witch trials). When these women were brought to the house Mary panicked and appeared to be in a terrified state. Strange things then began to happen:

> It was also deposed that strange noises, as of whistling, scratching, etc., were heard in the house, and that a sulphureous smell was observed in the rooms; that stones, turf, and the like were thrown about the house, and the coverlets, etc., frequently taken off the beds and made up in the shape of a corpse; and that a bolster once walked out of a room into the kitchen with a night-gown about it!...in some of her fits three strong men were scarcely able to hold her in the bed; and at that time she vomited feathers, cotton yarn, pins, and buttons; and that on one occa-sion she slid off the bed and was laid on the floor, as if supported and drawn by an invincible power.

Such bizarre testimony did not convince the jury, but the judge thought otherwise, and sentenced the accused women to a year in prison and four sessions in the pillory, where one of them lost an eye.

One particular class of auditory haunting, not so commonly reported today as in past centuries, involves what Owen Davies has called "occupational sounds," where the ghost is identified by making the noises that were associated with their job when they were alive. For example a man from Longtown in Hertfordshire, England, described how he had heard the ghost of a hurdle-maker (hurdles are portable wooden frames mainly used as temporary fences) "tap, tap, tap, choppin' wood for his hurdles all about the place where he was used to work." In the 1930s, in the village of Berwick St. James in Wiltshire, the site of a carpenter's workshop was plagued by the tapping sounds of the former occupant's hammer. The many knocking or tapping noises reported from mines, often associated with a type of subterranean fairy known under various names, such as "knockers" in the tin mines of Cornwall, "coblynau" in Wales and "kobolds" in Germany, are also related to this kind of haunting.

The annals of ghost lore are full of tales of mysterious footsteps, for some reason often connected with tragic deaths. In her article for the *California Folklore Quarterly* for April 1942, Rosalie Hankey recounts tales of ghostly moans, groans, and footsteps connected with the Mining Building of the University of California. One story related by Hankey describes a professor and his assistant who often had to work late into the night in the Mining Building. The two academics reported that they would hear footsteps approach the closed door and expect to see a fellow instructor enter. However, though the door would always open, no one would come in. The assistant tried to follow the footsteps on a number of occasions, but was never able to discover anything. Hankey was told by more than one informant that the strange occurrences in the

Mining Building were caused by the spirit of a soldier who had been killed or committed suicide when staying in the building during the time of the First World War. However, when Hankey checked the Berkeley city records for 1914–1919, she found no record of any suicide, murder, or serious injury at the Mining Building during this period. A similar tale is recounted by Anne Bradford and Barrie Roberts in their book of English hauntings *Strange Meetings* (2002). In this story, which took place in a house in Red Lion Street, Alvechurch, Worcestershire, the informant told the authors that when in the house they would often hear "the front door open and close, then footsteps going down the passageway to the kitchen." A man from the village told the informant that the people who used to live in the house had a son who had been killed driving a tank in World War II. It was believed that the times when the footsteps were heard coincided with the periods when the son would have been home on leave.

Another story of unexplained footsteps told to Bradford and Roberts appeared in their *Midland Spirits and Spectres* (1998). The incident occurred in 1/351 Bridge Street West, Hockley in Birmingham in 1952. One Saturday evening, the informant's husband was climbing the stairs when he heard footsteps come from the bottom of the stairs and run past him to the top. When the same thing happened the following Saturday night the man decided to connect a two-way light on the stairs, and after he did so, for some reason there were no more phantom footsteps. A few months later the husband bought a copy of the local newspaper, the *Birmingham Evening Mail*, and read an account of a man who had been sent to prison for strangling his wife some time earlier. Apparently, after hearing in a local pub that his wife had been carrying on with a neighbor, the man had rushed home, ran up the stairs, and murdered her. The address of the house was 1/351 Bridge Street West.

Phantom music is another fairly frequent occurrence in ghost lore, and has parallels with tales from the west of England and elsewhere of "fairy music," used to entice mortals into fairy hills or subterranean dwellings. One of the cases (Case 10) collected by Sir Ernest Bennett for his *Apparitions and Haunted Houses* (1939) describes phantom music from a public road, near a church yard, in a village in southern Scotland. One witness, a minister who had heard the strange music on a number of occasions, described the most recent performance thus in a letter from July 1889:

> When I had reached the usual spot, there burst upon my ear, from the direction of the churchyard, what seemed to be the splendid roll of a full brass and reed band...I never for a moment doubted its reality...I walked on, enjoying it thoroughly, never dreaming that I was not listening to good ordinary music, till it suddenly struck me that the sound, though now faint, ought to have been inaudible, as there was now between me and the churchyard the big, broad shoulder of S. (a hill)...and though not superstitious enough to believe that there was anything which could not be explained on natural grounds, I felt that the explanation was beyond my power of discovery or conjecture.

Another witness to otherworldly music from the same area around the churchyard was a "Lady Z," who wrote to Bennett of her experience on a hot afternoon of July 12, 1888:

> I was sitting resting with some old ladies at our pretty little cemetery chapel...Whilst I was talking I stopped suddenly exclaiming, 'Listen! what is that singing?' It was the most beautiful singing I had ever heard, just a wave of cathedral chanting, a great many voices, which only lasted a few seconds...There

were several others sitting with us, but they heard nothing (which astonished me).

When the lady later told her husband of the experience, she expected to be rebuffed with a down-to-earth explanation for the singing. However, he replied that he had often heard "chanting" before from the same place. Lady Z thought the voices she heard "could not have been human," and described the music she heard as "heavenly," though it is indeed curious that those sitting with her at the chapel did not hear anything.

The majority of instances of ghostly voices quoted in Owen Davies's *The Haunted: A Social History of Ghosts* (2007) were ingenious hoaxes, often created using ventriloquism. On one occasion in the 1760s, a French ventriloquist known as Monsieur Saint-Gille was sheltering in a monastery during a thunderstorm, where he found the monks mourning the death of one of their brethren. While Saint-Gille was being shown the tomb of the deceased he threw his voice to make it seem as if the spirit of the dead monk was speaking from the sky above them. The ghostly voice criticized the monks for not doing more to send his soul more rapidly to heaven and the astonished friars immediately arranged a mass to pray for the monk's soul. A simpler trick was used in another French case from the 1580s, when a long hollow reed was inserted through a wall close to the bed of a woman, through which a man-servant spoke mimicking the voice of her dead husband. The same idea was utilized around 1603 to cheat a widow in Cannington, Somerset, England, out of her estate. On this occasion the voice told her to pass on her estate to a "special friend" rather than to her son, otherwise "the devil would carry her off to Hell."

Nowadays phantom voices are usually associated with Electronic Voice Phenomena—or EVP. Briefly, this is where human sounding voices are heard on a recording, most often on audiotape, though not at the time of the recording, but afterward, when the tape is played back. These "voices" are often interpreted as proof that the spirits of the dead are attempting to communicate, much as spirit rappings were thought to be contact from the dead during the heyday of spiritualism. A recent (January 2007) nine-minute-long example of EVP from an old hotel in upstate New York is purported to be a recording of a horrific attack that took place there at some time in the past. Skeptics would argue that these supposed "voices," when not outright hoaxes, result from low-quality recording equipment, interference from the radio and CB radio transmissions, wireless baby minders, and the many millions of other electronic gadgets filling the air waves. Sound engineer David Federlein has criticized a basic mistake made by paranormal investigators when making EVP recordings, that of the tendency to adjust the sensitivity levels of their microphones to the highest level, thus raising the "noise floor"—the electrical noise created by all electrical devices—and consequently obtaining white noise. The resulting ghost voices are most likely people creating meaning out of what is essentially random noise, hearing what they would like to hear, which if you are a "ghost hunter," is a ghostly voice. Admittedly, some examples of EVP do sound rather eerie, and the phenomenon has not been explained to everyone's satisfaction.

A common belief in modern ghost lore is that if a smell is connected with a ghost, it often defines whether the spirit is good or evil—a pleasant smell, often of flowers, is associated with a friendly ghost, while a stale, rank odor is associated with an unpleasant or threatening phantom. These associations have parallels in medieval Christian biographies of saints, where angels and saints exuded sweet-smelling fragrances. However, scents connected with ghosts are rare until the mid-19th century and the arrival of spiritualism. It is curious that so few "olfactory ghosts" were reported up until the Victorian period, though its appearance during the heyday of spiritualism, when just about every form of communication from the dead imaginable was recorded, is perhaps understandable. In the 17th century, when smells were associated with the spirits of the dead at all, it was usually described in contemporary pamphlets as the sulphurous odor of brimstone, often connected with the Devil in popular lore. A much more offensive smell haunted the bedroom of a 17th-century English gentlewoman, which she decided to investigate and "opening the Bed, she smelt the smell of a Carcase some-while dead," though no one was there.

There are various accounts of unexplained odors in modern paranormal literature, often associated with a favorite hobby or pastime the "spirit" enjoyed while alive. Consequently, accounts of ghostly perfume, cigar smoke, and a particular kind of flowers favored by the deceased are common in tales of ghostly aromas. One article on the subject of ghostly aromas appeared on the *Suite101* Website in December 2000, and contains some fairly typical examples. One of the stories mentioned concerns a guest "in a certain California bed and breakfast that overlooks the ocean" who smelled cloves throughout the night. When she asked the manager about the smell the next morning she was told that some believed that the room was haunted by a woman who used to enjoy clove-flavored chewing gum. Another incident occurred when the author of the article and her daughter were attending a lecture on the subject of ghosts. During the talk the woman's daughter began to sneeze and "commented on the overpowering aroma of old fashioned lilac perfume that was permeating the room." They were later informed that lilacs had been a favorite of a young woman whose ghost was supposed to haunt the premises.

There are various medical conditions associated with "olfactory hallucinations." One is known as "Parosmia," and involves a distortion of the sense of smell, so that the affected person reports smelling something other than the scent which is present. Unexplained unpleasant smells are basic symptoms of this condition. Another disorder associated with the sense of smell is "Phantosmia," where there is no odor present but the affected person detects something. The smells vary from person to person, but can include rotting food, smoke, chlorine, perfume, and even fresh flowers. Phantosmia usually result from damage to the nervous tissue in the olfactory system, caused by viral infection, head trauma, surgery, and possibly exposure to particular toxins or use of certain drugs. The condition may also be a symptom of epilepsy. Many doctors are of the opinion that there are more sufferers from olfactory hallucinations than is generally realized, and such medical conditions must surely be taken into consideration before jumping to conclusions about ghostly smells being a form of communication from the spirit world.

Chapter 16

Poltergeists

The German word *poltergeist* roughly translates as "noisy spirit" or "noisy ghost." The poltergeist phenomenon has been described in English sources from the mid-16th century onward, but the first British writer to use the term *poltergeist* was Victorian writer Catherine Crowe, in her classic account of supernatural occurrences *The Night-side of Nature* (1848). Parapsychologists often refer to the poltergeist phenomenon using the rather unwieldy term *Recurrent Spontaneous Psychokinesis* (RSPK). A most notable point about poltergeist activity is that it has been described in different periods and over a large cross section of cultures as generally exhibiting the same characteristics. Some of the most common of these characteristics are: the movement and hurling around of inanimate, sometimes heavy, objects without apparent agent; the opening and closing of doors and windows by no visible means; unexplained noises such as voices, moans, screams, explosions, crashes, raps, thumps, scratches and knocks on floors, doors and walls; heavy footsteps; bed-shaking; the breaking of household objects such as crockery; the destruction of garments; the throwing of stones, rocks, and dirt; bad smells; mysterious fires; the appearance of pools of water on floors; the malfunctioning of electrical equipment; telephone ringing; the unexplained appearance of objects ("apports"); apparitions; and even physical assault (as in the case of Rumanian teenager Eleonore Zugun, investigated by the controversial Harry Price in the 1920s). Stone throwing often signals the arrival of a poltergeist, with victims testifying to a bombardment of stones or even bricks on the roofs and walls of their houses, seemingly from nowhere and sometimes lasting for days (or even weeks) before any other kind of unexplained phenomenon occurs.

First century Jewish historian Josephus describes phenomena connected with "possession" that would nowadays be attributed to poltergeist activity. Jacob Grimm, one of the brothers Grimm, writing in his *Deutsche Mythologie,* recounts a number of cases including one from Bingen-am-Rhein dated AD 355, where stones were thrown, people were pulled out of bed, and raps and loud noises were heard. Writing in his *Itinerarium Cambriae (*AD 1191) of his tour of Wales, clergyman and chronicler Giraldus Cambrensis describes an incident at a house in Pembrokeshire where "unclean spirits" threw dirt and other objects, garments were ripped and torn, and the "spirit" even spoke publicly of the various secrets of people present. These are not isolated cases; medieval chronicles are full of such incidents. The problem, however, with medieval and earlier accounts of poltergeist cases is that the incidents were not recorded as "history" as we know it today; the chronicles include records of many fantastical signs, wonders, and miracles and are thus not historical documents as such. Additionally, as the alleged incidents occurred in such remote periods, it is impossible now to check the genuineness or otherwise of the stories.

One of the most famous poltergeist cases is that of the "Tedworth Drummer" of England in 1661. In this case, a drum, which belonged to an imprisoned beggar called William Drury, proceeded to play on its own, accompanied by various other phenomena such as the hurling about of chairs, beds containing sleeping servants being lifted up, and loud scratching noises. The phenomena were believed by some to be the work of a demon magically sent by the drummer using the powers of witchcraft. The main source for the case is Joseph Glanvill's *Sadducismus Triumphatus* ("The Defeat of Sadducism"), written in 1668. This work argues for the existence of witchcraft and ghosts and their malign power, and criticizes those skeptical of the reality of such phenomena. One of the many poltergeist disturbances involving clergymen occurred at Epworth Rectory, Lincolnshire, England, in 1716–1717. The occupant at the time was Rev. Samuel Wesley, father of Methodist Church founder John Wesley, and his family. A record of the various knockings, raps, moving furniture, and other unexplained happenings can be found in the letters and notes of the family. The Wesleys named the ghost "Old Jeffrey," but the fact that most of the strange happenings centered around 19-year-old Hetty Wesley, one of seven Wesley daughters in the house, has persuaded some researchers, most notably Frank Podmore (1856–1910) of the Society for Psychical Research (SPR), that the poltergeist was nothing more than a hoax perpetuated by the Wesley children. Among the accounts of the phenomena written by family members there is, for some reason, nothing from Hetty, even though she was directly involved and often exhibited strange behavior during the disturbances. It should also be noted that some of the letters on which the fame of the case rests were written years after the purported events by John Wesley, who had been away at boarding school at the time the phenomena occurred and was well known for being both credulous and superstitious. Another possible explanation for the unexplained occurrences is that they were caused by disgruntled local people. As the eldest Wesley daughter, Emily, noted, the outbreak of strange activity began very soon after her father's preaching against folk religious practice in the parish. Enemies of the family had previously maimed some of the Wesleys' animals, and may have also caused the fires at the Rectory in 1702 and 1709.

A series of apparently bizarre and frightening incidents are alleged to have taken place on a Tennessee farm in 1817 and have become known as the "Bell Witch Haunting." The Bell Witch herself was thought by many to be the spirit of Kate Batts, one time neighbor of John Bell, owner of the farm where the disturbances took place, and who had apparently been involved in a dispute with him over land. The phenomena included apparitions of strange animals, whistling, disembodied voices, loud laughing and singing, and vicious physical assaults on people at the farm, which are claimed by some to have resulted in the death of John Bell. Unfortunately, the first public record of the alleged events did not appear until 1886, when it was mentioned in Albert Goodpasture's *History of Tennessee*, and it was not until 1894 that a full account of the case appeared— Martin Van Buren Ingram's *Authenticated History of the Bell Witch of Tennessee*. As with a number of the most famous poltergeist stories, no firsthand accounts exist of the Bell Witch Haunting. The famous "diary" of William Bell, who was only 6 years old at the time of the "haunting," and which is the document upon which much of the information of the case derives, was allegedly written 25 years later. However, many researchers doubt that the diary ever existed as no record of it has ever been found, and some believe it to be an invention of Martin Van Buren Ingram.

Two interesting and controversial modern poltergeist cases are the "Enfield Poltergeist" and the "Mackenzie Poltergeist." The former took place in 1977 in a north London council house, occupied by a single mother with her four children. The phenomena included the usual array of moving furniture, knockings on the walls, spontaneous fires, pools of water materializing on the floor, cold breezes, physical assaults, the appearance of graffiti, equipment malfunction and failure, and various items being thrown around the house. Initial investigations by Maurice Grosse and Guy Lyon Playfair of the SPR found considerable evidence for genuine unexplained phenomena, though further investigations by Anita Gregory and John Beloff, also of the SPR, came to the conclusion that the "poltergeist" phenomena had been faked by the children. Indeed, one of the children, Janet, admitted to Gregory that they had been responsible for at least some of the supposedly "paranormal" occurrences, though not all. The case remains controversial to this day.

The alarming series of events that make up the Mackenzie Poltergeist case took place in 1999 in Greyfriars Kirkyard, Edinburgh. It is alleged that the poltergeist events in the area were triggered by a homeless man spending the night in a mausoleum belonging to Sir George Mackenzie, who died in 1691, and was known during his lifetime for his bloody persecution of the Covenanters, a powerful Scottish Presbyterian movement. The homeless man accidentally caused some damage to Mackenzie's coffin, and was subsequently witnessed running and screaming in terror from the site, to be found later in a state of delirium by police. Since that strange night, weird phenomena have been reported in the kirkyard and the surrounding area. Neighboring houses were apparently plagued by objects flying around the rooms and crockery smashing, while visitors to the site itself experienced feelings of extreme heat or cold, suffered cuts and bruises from an unknown assailant, had their throats squeezed, coats tugged violently, and were, on occasion, even knocked unconscious by an invisible force. As in many poltergeist cases, subsequent exorcisms of the area failed to halt the phenomena.

In many 17th- and 18th-century poltergeist cases, such as The Tedworth Drummer and the Bell Witch, the disturbances were, at the time, attributed to witchcraft. Indeed, in the Tedworth case the drummer was eventually found guilty of witchcraft and transported for the offense. From the beginning of the 16th century to the middle of the 18th, in Western Europe (the Early Modern Period), the differences between the various classes of supernatural creatures was often blurred, with elementals, ghosts, apparitions, demons and witches all being equally blamed for causing poltergeist-like effects. One very obvious characteristic of poltergeist behavior is how much it resembles the mischievous conduct of traditional creatures of folklore. In English tales, certain types of fairies known as boggarts and hobgoblins, the former a common name in the northern counties of England for any frightening supernatural being, would knock, throw stones, break dishes, and generally annoy people. "Old Nancy" was such a creature known from the village of Mixon in Staffordshire, and she would rap on the table and the wainscoting in a manner often reported in poltergeist cases. Similar to the poltergeist, the boggart was often attached to a particular household. The best known anecdote about these troublesome creatures was once told in the English northern counties as well as in Lincolnshire and Shropshire. This story describes a farmer and his family whose house was so tormented by the incessant tricks of a boggart that they decided to move. As they were leaving a neighbor asked if they really were moving for good. "Yes, we're moving," said the farmer. "Yes indeed," echoed the boggart's voice from an old milk churn in one of the carts, "we're *all* moving." Realizing they could never escape the creature, the family returned to their house, the farmer saying they might as well be tormented in their own house as anywhere else.

But does the poltergeist exist outside of demonology and folklore? And if so, what causes it? The vast majority of poltergeist incidents can be explained in terms of a hoax, overactive imagination, perceptual error, cumulative exaggerations, and sometimes even hysterical self-deception, though a few cases (the Mackenzie case is one example) do not presently appear to fit these explanations. The most popular theory put forward for "genuine" poltergeist activity is that it is caused unwittingly by a human agent, usually a teenage girl perhaps undergoing some emotional trauma. Some psychical researchers believe that a troubled adolescent unconsciously manipulates objects using psychokinesis (PK), a type of energy allegedly generated in the brain. In other words, the teenager is an unconscious "medium." According to researchers at the Rhine Research Center Institute for Parapsychology at Duke University, Durham, North Carolina, poltergeist activity is the physical expression of psychological trauma. The problem here is that the existence of PK has never been proven, and so we are in danger of attempting to explain one unknown with another. There are also a number of poltergeist cases in which those involved have no psychological problems at all, and where there are no adolescents in the household. How can we explain these? A further point is that there are millions of troubled teenagers all over the world, but the vast majority do not cause poltergeist activity to occur.

Natural phenomena that are often the cause of what appears to be a poltergeist disturbance include static electricity and electromagnetic fields. Electromagnetic Interference (EMI) has been found to be behind at least one supposed poltergeist investigated by Midlands (UK) investigation group Paraseach, and there is an increasing amount of evidence to show that it could explain many more cases. However, electromagnetic interference does not explain how enough power is generated to move objects such as heavy pieces of furniture, or to shower a room with stones, make objects appear from nowhere, or start fires. But it must be born in mind that accounts of such unexplained phenomena allegedly caused by poltergeist activity are often grossly exaggerated, or even completely false, especially those recorded during the 16th to 18th centuries, so there is really no need to explain the more extreme phenomena described in such cases. The function of the poltergeist visitation during this period, especially when described by a clergyman, was to prove to non-believers that demonic forces actually existed, and by inference that a spiritual hierarchy of demons, spirits, and angels, with God at the top, must then also exist.

Other researchers, especially those involved in the spiritualist movement of the mid- to late-19th century, have suggested that "spirit entities" are responsible for the phenomena; perhaps generating the power by attaching themselves to suitably disturbed teenagers. But the very nature of these hypothetical "spirits" means that scientifically at least, they cannot be investigated, which is perhaps just as well. Nevertheless, the inability to find a convincing scientific explanation for the phenomenon, the significant amount of poltergeist cases exhibiting similar characteristics occurring during long period of time in widely different cultures, have made the poltergeist one of the most enduring of unexplained mysteries. What is certain is that, in past centuries when mischievous activity occurred around the house, it was attributed to demons, witches, and fairies. Now, in our technologically obsessed materialistic world of the 21st century, the same activity is being investigated as a physical reality by hoards of ghost hunting groups equipped with video cameras, digital recorders, and EMF detectors. In the 16th to 19th centuries the poltergeist could be said to have had a social and/or religious function, today it is up to those investigating modern cases of alleged poltergeists to prove the phenomenon is anything more than modern folklore.

𝔅ibliography

Aldhouse-Green, Stephen. "Great Sites: Paviland Cave." British Archaeology Website *www.britarch.ac.uk/ba/ba61/feat3.shtml* (accessed May, 2008).

Allred, Grover C. "Notes on the Appearance of a Spectral Death Messenger". Western Folklore 19 (1960): 197–199.

Anderson, John Q. "The Legend of the Phantom Coach in East Texas". *Western Folklore* 22 (1963): 259–262.

Anon. "The Woman in White: A Ghost." *Western Folklore* 6, (1947): 184–185.

Ari Berk and William Spytma. "Penance, Power, and Pursuit: On the Trail of the Wild Hunt." The Endicott Studio Website. *www.endicott-studio.com/rdrm/forhunt.html* (accessed May 6, 2008).

Arzy, S, M. Seeck, S. Ortique, L. Spinelli, and O. Blanke. "Induction of an Illusory Shadow Person." *Nature* 443: 287.

Beardsley, Richard K. and Rosalie Hankey. "The Vanishing Hitchhiker", *California Folklore Quarterly* 1 (1942): 303–335.

Beck, Jane C. "The White Lady of Great Britain and Ireland," *Folklore* 81 (1970): 292–306.

Bennett, Gillian. "Ghost and Witch in the Sixteenth and Seventeenth Centuries." *Folklore* 97 (1986): 3–14.

Bennett, Gillian. "The Vanishing Hitchhiker at Fifty-Five." *Western Folklore* 57 (1998): 1–17.

Bennett, Sir Ernest. *Apparitions and Haunted Houses*. London, Faber and Faber Ltd. 1939.

Beyer, Jürgen. "On the Transformation of Apparition Stories in Scandinavia and Germany, c.1350-1700." *Folklore* 110 (1999): 39–47.

Biggs S. J. M (Mrs). "Headless Ghosts." *Folklore* 50 (1939): 98.

Blaschke, Jayme. "Headless skeleton expands understanding of ancient Andean rituals." Texas State University Website. *www.txstate.edu/news/news_releases/news_archive/2007/05/Conlee053107.html* (accessed May 1, 2008).

———. *Midland Spirits and Spectres*. Warwick, UK: Quercus Publications, 1998.

Bradford, Anne. *Worcestershire Ghosts and Hauntings*. Redditch, Worcestershire, UK: Hunt End Books, 2001.

Bradford, Anne, and Barrie Roberts. *Strange Meetings*. Warwick, UK: Quercus Publications, 2002.

Briggs, Katherine. *A Dictionary of Fairies*. Harmondsworth, Middlesex, UK: Penguin Books Ltd. 1977.

Brooks, J.A. *Ghosts of London*. Norwich, UK: Jarrold Publishing, 1991.

Brown, Theo. "The Black Dog." *Folklore* 69 (958): 175–192.

Bibliography

————. "Some Examples of Post-Reformation Folklore in Devon." *Folklore* 72 (1961): 388-399.

————. *Devon Ghosts.* Norwich, UK: Jarrold Publishing, 1982.

Brunvand, Jan Harold. *The Vanishing Hitchhiker: Urban Legends and their Meanings.* London: Picador, 1983.

Burchell, Simon. *Phantom Black Dogs in Latin America,* Loughborough, UK: Heart of Albion Press, 2007.

"California Legends. Celebrity and Infamous Ghosts of America." Legends of America Website. *www.legendsofamerica.com/GH-CelebrityGhosts.html* (accessed May 1, 2008).

Carrington, H., and N. Fodor. *The Story of the Poltergeist Down the Centuries.* London: Rider & Co. 1953.

Carroll, Robert Todd. Skeptic's Dictionary—Electronic Voice Phenomenon (EVP). *http://skepdic.com/evp.html.* (accessed May 1, 2008).

Çatalhöyük Excavations. Çatalhöyük Website. *www.catalhoyuk.com* (accessed May 1, 2008).

Chambers, Paul. "All in the Mind." The Association for the Scientific Study of Anomalous Phenomena (ASSAP) Website. *www.assap.org/newsite/articles/Mind.html.* (accessed May 1, 2008).

Clarke, D., and A. Roberts. "Heads and Tales: The Screaming Skull Legends of Britain" *Fortean Studies* 3 (1996): 126-59.

Davies, Jonathan Ceredig. *Folklore of West and Mid Wales.* Lampeter, Wales, UK: Llanerch Press 1992, (1911).

Davies, Owen. *The Haunted: A Social History of Ghosts.* New York, Palgrave Macmillan, 2007.

"De-Mystifying the 'Marfa Lights.'" *http://godshome.us/marfa/MarfaLights.html* (accessed May 1, 2008).

Devereux, Paul. *Haunted Land.* London: Piatkus, 2001.

Evans, Hilary. *Visions, Apparitions, Alien Visitors: A Comparative Study of the Entity Enigma.* London: Book Club Associates, 1984.

Feilberg, H. F. "Ghostly Lights." *Folklore* 6 (1895): 288–300.

Finucane, R.C. *Appearances of the Dead. A Cultural History of Ghosts*. London: Junction books, 1982.

Gauld, A. and T. Cornell. *Poltergeists*. London: Routledge & Kegan Paul, 1979.

Goss, Michael. *The Evidence for Phantom Hitch-Hikers*. Wellingborough, Northamptonshire, UK: Aquarian Press, 1984

Green, Celia, and Charles McCreery. *Apparitions*. New York: St. Martin's Press. 1975.

Gundarsson, Kveldulf Hagen. "The Folklore of the Wild Hunt and the Furious Host." Mountain Thunder Website, Issue 7, Winter 1992. *www.vinland.org/heathen/mt/wildhunt.html* (accessed May 7, 2008).

Hankey, Rosalie. "California Ghosts." *California Folklore Quarterly* 1 (1942): 155–177.

Hauck, Dennis William. *The International Directory of Haunted Places*. New York, Penguin Books, 2000.

Haunted Connecticut. "Black Dog of the Hanging Hills, Meriden, Connecticut." Haunted Connecticut Website. *www.geocities.com/hauntedCT/hanginghills.htm* (accessed May 1, 2008).

Haunted Houses. *www.hauntedhouses.com* (accessed May 1, 2008).

Henderson, Jan-Andrew. *The Ghost that Haunted Itself: The Story of the McKenzie Poltergeist*. Edinburgh, Scotland: Mainstream Publishing, 2001.

Hole, Christina. *Haunted England*. London: Fitzhouse Books, 1990 (1940).

Hope Robbins, Rossell. "The Imposture of Witchcraft." *Folklore* 74 (1963): 545–562.

Houston, Susan Hilary. "Ghost Riders in the Sky," *Western Folklore* 23 (1964): 153–162.

Bibliography

Ingram, John H. *The Haunted Homes and Family Traditions of Great Britain*. London: Reeves and Turner, 1912.

Jacobson, Laurie, and Marc Wanamaker. *Hollywood Haunted: A Ghostly Tour of Filmland*. Santa Monica, Calif.:, Angel City Press, 1999.

Jones, Louis C. "Hitchhiking Ghosts in New York." *California Folklore Quarterly* 3 (1944): 284–292.

———. "The Ghosts of New York: An Analytical Study." *The Journal of American Folklore* 57 (1944): 237–254.

Kirk, Robert. *The Secret Commonwealth of Elves, Fauns and Fairies*. Stirling, Scotland, Eneas MacKay, 1933 (1691).

Kittredge, George Lyman. "Disenchantment by Decapitation." *The Journal of American Folklore* 18 (1905): 1–14.

MacKenzie, Andrew. *Hauntings and Apparitions*. London: Heinemann Ltd, 1982.

Maclagan, R.C. "Ghost Lights of the West Highlands." *Folklore* 8 (1897): 203–256.

Mysterious Britain. "Ghosts and Hauntings in Britain—Screaming Skulls."*www.mysteriousbritain.co.uk/hauntings/screaming_skulls.html* (accessed May 1, 2008).

———. "The Folklore of the British Isles—Phantom Black Dogs." Mysterious Britain Website. *www.mysteriousbritain.co.uk/folklore/black_dogs.html* (accessed May 1, 2008).

Norman, Michael, and Beth Scott. *Haunted Heritage: A Definitive Collection of North American Ghost Stories*. New York: Tor Books, 2002.

Oberding, Janice. "I Smell a Ghost." *www.suite101.com/article.cfm/ghosts_and_haunted_spots/55403* (accessed May 1, 2008).

Owen, A.R.G. *Can We Explain the Poltergeist?* New York: Garrett Publications. 1964.

Owen, Harold. *Journey From Obscurity, Memoirs of the Owen Family*. London: Oxford University Press, 1963.

Parsons, Coleman O. "Association of the White Lady with Wells." Foklore 44 (1933): 295–305.

Partridge Smith, Grace. "Folklore from 'Egypt.'" *The Journal of American Folklore* 54 (1941) 48–59.

Pausanias. *Guide to Greece*. London: Penguin Books, 1979.

Playfair, G. L. *This House is Haunted: An Investigation into the Enfield Poltergeist*. London: Souvenir Press. 1980.

Raudive, Konstantin. *Breakthrough: An Amazing Experiment in Electronic Communication with the Dead*. New York: Taplinger Publishing Company, 1971.

Rodger, Ian. "The Headless Horseman: An Amateur Inquiry." *Journal of the Folklore Institute* 2 (1965) 266–271.

Roll, W.G. *The Poltergeist*. Nelson Doubleday Inc, Garden City, N.Y.: Double Day, 1972.

Rudkin, Ethel H. "The Black Dog." *Folklore* 49(1938): 111–131.

Salleh, Anna. "Mystery of the Min Min Lights Explained." *www.abc.net.au/science/news/stories/s818193.htm* (accessed May 1, 2008).

Sandburg, Carl. *Abraham Lincoln: The Prairie Years*. New York, Harcourt, Brace and Co., 1926. pp.423–4.

Sean Tudor. "The Ghost of Blue Bell Hill". Road Ghosts Website. *www.roadghosts.com/blue%20bell%20hill.htm* (accessed May 16, 2008).

Seymour, Miranda. *Mary Shelley*. London: John Murray, 2000.

Sicard, Cheri. "Hollywood's Most Famous Ghosts." Fabulous Travel Website. *www.fabuloustravel.com/ww/haunthollywood/haunthollywood.html* (accessed May 1, 2008).

Sidgwick, E. E. Gurney, F.W.H Myers, and F. Podmore. *Phantasms of the Living*, New York: University Books, 1962.

Simpson, Jacqueline, and Steve Roud. *A Dictionary of English Folklore*. Oxford, Oxford University Press 2000.

Bibliography

Sitwell, S. *Poltergeists: Fact or Fancy.* New York: Dorset Press. 1988 (1959).

Spencer, J. *The Encyclopedia of Ghosts and Spirits.* London: Headline Book Publishing, 1992.

Spencer, J., and A. Spencer. *The Poltergeist Phenomenon.* London: Headline, 1996.

St. Leger-Gordon, Ruth E. *Witchcraft & Folklore of Dartmoor.* New York: Bell Publishing Company, 1972.

Taylor, David. "Spaces of Transition: New Light on the Haunted House." *www.indigogroup.co.uk/edge/spaces.htm* (accessed May 1, 2008).

"The Brown Mountain Lights website." *www1.appstate.edu/dept/physics/caton/BML/BML.htm* (accessed May 1, 2008)

Thiselton-Dyer, T.F. *Ghost World.* Middlesex, UK: Senate, 2000 (1893).

Tom Nicholson. "Levo´a's ghosts." The Slovak Spectator Website. *http://travel.spectator.sk/ss2006/03_levoca.html* (accessed May 1, 2008).

Trevelyan, Marie. *Folk-lore and Folk-Stories of Wales.* Wakefield, UK: EP Publishing, 1973 (1909).

Trubshaw, Bob. "Black dogs in folklore." At the Edge magazine Website. *www.indigogroup.co.uk/edge/bdogfl.htm* (accessed May 1, 2008).

———. *Explore Phantom Black Dogs.* Loughborough, UK: Heart of Albion Press, 2005.

Tyrrell, G.N.M. *Apparitions.* London: Gerald Duckworth and Co. Ltd., 1953.

Wagner, Stephen. "What you need to know about Electronic Voice Phenomena." About.com: Paranormal Phenomena Website. *http://paranormal.about.com/library/weekly/aa020303a.htm* (acessed May 1, 2008).

Walhouse, M.J. "Ghostly Lights." *Folklore* 5 (1894): 293—299.

Ward, Donald (ed). *The German Legends of the Brothers Grimm.* London: Millington Books, 1981.

Weird New Jersey. "Road Less Traveled: Clinton Road." *www.weirdnj.com/stories/_roads02.asp* (accessed May 1, 2008).

Welker, Bill. De-Mystifying the Marfa Lights Website: *http://godshome/us/marfa/MarfaLights.html* (accessed May 1, 2008).

Westropp, Thos. J. "Folklore Survey of County Clare." *Folklore* 21 (1910): 180–199.

Westwood, Jennifer. *Albion: A Guide to Legendary Britain.* London: Book Club Associates, 1986.

Westwood, Jennifer, and Jacqueline Simpson. *The Lore of the Land: A Guide to England's Legends, from Spring-heeled Jack to the Witches of Warboys.* London: Penguin Books Ltd, 2005.

Wianwright, Martin. "Roman soldiers march on M6, Britain's most haunted road." *http://www.guargian.co.uk/uk/2006/oct/31/britishidentity.martinwainwright* (accessed May 1, 2008).

Wilson, C. *Poltergeist! A Study in Destructive Haunting.* Sevenoaks, Kent, UK: New English Library, 1981.

Witcutt, W.P. "Notes on Staffordshire Folklore." *Folklore* 53 (1942): 126–127.

Wuensch, Dr. Karl L., "Parosmia and Phantosmia." Dr. Wuensch's Anosmia Website: *http://personal.ecu.edu/wuenschk/parosmia.htm* (accessed May 1, 2008).

Yeats, W.B (ed). *Fairy and Folk Tales of the Irish Peasantry.* London: Walter Scott, nd.

Index

Lore of the Ghost

Index

About the Author

Brian Haughton was born in Birmingham, United Kingdom, and is a graduate of Nottingham (BA in Archaeology) and Birmingham (M. Phil in Greek Archaeology) Universities. He has worked on archaeological projects in England and Greece, and is an author and researcher on the subjects of prehistoric archaeology, sacred places, mythology, and supernatural folklore. Haughton's first book, *Hidden History: Lost Civilizations, Secret Knowledge, and Ancient Mysteries* was published in January 2007 (Career Press, Inc.), and has already been translated into seven languages. His second publication *Haunted Spaces, Sacred Places*, was published by New Page Books in July 2008.

Haughton's work has been featured in various print publications across the world including *Doorways* magazine, *Awareness*, and *All Destiny* and on Websites such as the B.B.C's *Legacies, World Mysteries,* and the *Book of Thoth.* He is a member of the Folklore Society (England) and serves as a consultant for United Kingdom-based research and investigative organization Parasearch. Haughton long ago fell for the lure of the ancient and the supernatural, initially inspired by visiting the Neolithic chambered tombs of the Cotswold Hills in England and by reading the ghost stories of Sheridan Le Fanu and M.R. James.